WOMEN

by

Dave Sim and Gerhard

Aardvark-Vanaheim Inc.
First printing: (limited signed and numbered) April 1994
Second printing: April 1994
Third printing: March 1995

ISBN 0-919359-14-0

Printed in Windsor, Ontario by
Preney Print & Litho Inc.

PRINTED IN CANADA

Dave's dedication:

To the Gender Opposite as the Chasm Widens:

no hard feelings, eh?

Gerhard's dedication:

To Scott, Eric & Frank The Boys In The Band.

Introduction:

Mothers and Daughters continues in this, the second volume of the four volume series. As I write these words, I am edging closer and closer to the core of the Cerebus story-line. Books three and four (if I am able to do the central idea justice) will come as close as anything I have written to expressing reality as I see it. I am edging around my subject, encircling it, containing it with a loose network of ideas and concepts. There is a recoil effect in writing these things: a psychic backlash which I anticipated and which I am unable to escape. The laws governing action and reaction seem to be universal even (maybe especially) in the realm of creativity.

As I look back on *Women,* it is with a sense of loss for a subject which I found effortless. Structurally, each of the four books in the series say the same thing, but they say it in very different ways. *Women* was entirely episodic. It could be read strictly as entertainment or it could be examined more closely for its underlying and interwoven message: 'Does this seem right to you?' Certainly the *Cerebus* series itself, my on-going portrayal of the war between mothers and daughters, Cirinists and Kevillists, has provoked an outpouring of comment and criticism which only occasionally has centered on the story points being made. 'Does this seem right to you?' Even the question itself is interpreted in such a variety of ways, most of them evasive, that I am quite content with what was being said in these pages. I was able to maintain a distance from the subject being addressed. Here, what do you think of this? I think the Oprah Winfrey parody was that part that was the most fun for me. I had to watch the show several times to get Rap 'ho'e (a name which I was, regrettably, unable to shoehorn into the proceedings) distilled down to a visual essence. It was one of those occasions when it was genuinely impossible to do a parody of something. The best I could hope for was to capture the essence of the genre and let the portrayal stand as self-evident humour. The key element? That there *was* no essence to the genre; the trappings themselves were all that it had to say. Here is an audience full of normal people who are very concerned. Here is a host who is very concerned. Here are the victims and perpetrators who are very concerned. Here is the expert psychologist who is very concerned. The Importance of Being Earnest sums up what passes for the thematic core. We care. We all care. We want to help. We will weep collective tears. We will share a communal laugh. When we hear something which reflects our inherent decency, we will applaud wildly. We are of one flesh here, we are of one mind. When we all think the same way, something inherently good has been achieved. We are empowered. There are moments of discord, we feel ourselves dividing. A platitude is enunciated. We all applaud. The discord is gone. The power is back.

I created an unexpected joke in the title of this volume. It's all Ger and I can do to keep from laughing when the advance phone orders come in. 'I'd like to order *Women*.' (hey, wouldn't we all?) 'Can you tell me when *Women* will be available?' (my guess would be when Hell freezes over) 'What's the price on *Women*?' (the bounty varies from state to state and is strictly illegal in Canada, I'm afraid).

I wish I could end this introduction with some kind of platitude about the War Between the Sexes. I wish I had some pithy little 'feel-good-homily-of-the-year' that would cause you all to break into a furious foot-stomping ovation with tears and hugs all around. I wish I could somehow snap my fingers and make everything okay. I wish I could look back on my adult life, post-1970, and say something more optimistic than 'if feminism hadn't come along I never would have become this isolated, this distanced from human society and I would have felt no need to do three hundred issues of *Cerebus*.' That isolation is so central to who I am and has been so critical to whatever progress I have made as an artist, writer and publisher, I can't even begin to conceive of where another path might have led me. For me, the trade-off has been more than sufficient: a one dollar lottery ticket that won the biggest jackpot in history.

Whoever you are, reading these words, either just after publication in spring of 1994, over the summer convention season, in 1996 (as half of the *Mothers & Daughters* story-line collected into four volumes, in 2005 (as the second longest 'novel' in the *Cerebus* project), I can only hope that you are half as happy with the cards you've been dealt as I am.

And to that smattering of half-hearted applause, I'll leave you now to *Mothers & Daughters* book two: *Women* as I make my way downstairs to the drawing board and pages four and five of issue 183 (pages 164 and 165 of book three: *Reads)*.

See you back here next year.

Dave Sim
Kitchener, Ontario
March 31, 1994

book two
women

The penis is an organ without scruple, without humanity, without common sense. Those women who understand this fact and make use of it have at their command all the resources of the modern world. I first had sexual congress at the age of fourteen with a high-placed government official in my native Lower Felda. He had pursued me, despite (or, rather, I suspect because of) my extreme youth for a period of several months. I was drawn very much to the power that he wielded within that government. I was attracted, however, not as a would-be lifemate, potential concubine or wife-to-be. Rather, I was drawn as someone who desired that same power for herself, as a means of instituting societal change for my own betterment and for the betterment of those elements of female society with which I was (and am) sympathetic. I presented my decision to him in the form of a bargain. He would answer all of the questions that I had about achieving, maintaining and using power and in exchange (once I was satisfied with his answers), his unscrupulous organ would be free to do with me as it would. We had a series of five meetings, each of several hours duration. I took meticulous notes, asked for clarification where I lacked understanding of the subject matter and began to get the first sketchy impressions of the parameters and dimensions of the task which lay before me. Once satisfied that I had learned all that this particular individual had to teach me, I then fulfilled my half of the bargain. The act itself took only slightly longer than eight minutes. I cleaned myself thoroughly, dressed and left his apartments. I had retained many of his letters of earnest entreaty and when (as I knew he would) he attempted to renew our relationship, I threatened him with exposure as a pederast. He ceased his unwanted attentions and I began my political career.

Astoria
Kevillist Origins

Great tolerance must be exercised when dealing with daughters. It is very difficult for a mother to recall that confused and turbulent time in her life when existence is profoundly unfocussed and a girl feels very strongly all the myriad forces which exert themselves upon her; both external forces and, more perniciously, her own tendency to submit herself and her will to that which is transient, attractive, compelling and ill-advised. Childbirth is the Goddess' greatest gift to womankind wherein an ordered mind supplants a disordered one; reality breaks through the thin membrane of interwoven and convoluted illusion which is a girl's consciousness to that point. Suddenly genuine purpose and True Womanhood make of her a contributing member of society, where previously she had been merely a discordant and willful obstruction to all that is ordered and healthy. The birth of a child takes the mother out of her own limited and self-absorbed vanity and shows her, clearly and in a way which will brook no denial, what the Goddess' purpose for her is. The irrational rage of the young girl who is reminded of this fact is proof positive that within her, at the core of her essential being, a True Voice is speaking always to her; reminding her that it is her destiny to bring forth new life; to care for it and to nurture it. When a daughter rails against this nature, the wise mother is silent and leaves it to the True Voice within the daughter to work its sweet magic on its own timetable, as it surely will. Time is always on the side of that True Voice.

Cirin
The New Matriarchy

Astoria:
No. Listen to what I'm saying. Move your fingers down the lock of hair. A little bit more. Hold it right there. Now tilt the fingers down. Loosen your wrist. You're fighting me. Tilt your fingers down toward the earlobe. A little bit more . . . no, that's too much. There. Like that.

Hairdresser:
(sighing) This is going to take forever.

Astoria:
It's going to take a lot longer than that if you don't listen to what I'm saying. Pay attention.

Hairdresser:
Yes, ma'am.

Astoria:
Turn your hand so that I can see how much hair you've got. Other way. All right. Now, cut the lock of hair on the other side of your fingers. No. No. In a straight line at the same angle as your fingers. Why do you think I told you what angle to hold your fingers at?

Hairdresser:
I . . . like this?

Astoria:
I asked you a question.

Hairdresser:
I . . . I'm sorry.

Astoria:
Follow the angle of your fingers. The scissors should be resting right against your . . . right against them. Flat against them. There. Yes. Like that.

Hairdresser:
Should I cut now.

Astoria:
Yes.

Astoria:
Now take your hand away so I can check how the . . . how it . . . That's good. That's fine.

Hairdresser:
Is it okay?

Astoria:
I just said it was. Okay, now move your hand back along the hair-line. No no. Not that high up. Here. Feel where my index finger is. My index finger. The one right next to the thumb. Pull a lock of hair exactly the same width right there. Don't tilt your fingers quite that much. A little bit less than you did on the first lock. Okay. Same idea; put the scissors flat against . . . that's it. Now you've got it. And cut.

Hairdresser:
Like this?

Astoria:
Okay. Take your hand away and let me see again. It's . . . well, it's not as good as the first one, is it?

Hairdresser:
I . . . I'm sorry.

Astoria:
Don't apologise; improve. Okay, now feel where my index finger is now. This time you're going to take a slightly wider lock of hair. *Slightly* wider. You've got a whole handful there . . .

Clerk:
You're so lucky to have the figure that you do . . . it's just perfect for today's fashions.

Astoria:
Thank you.

Clerk:
Do you mind if I ask what your secret is?

Astoria:
Not at all. I chain myself in a dark cell for months on end and eat only one meal a day consisting of stale mouldy bread and rancid vegetable soup.

Clerk:
Oh! I . . . well, I'm sure . . . oh, now that's a lovely blouse isn't it?

Astoria:
Except for the dropped stitches across the neckline and the loose button in the middle, it's wonderful.

Clerk:
Oh! I hadn't . . . well, we could fix that in a jiffy, I'm sure.

Astoria:
Do you sell a lot of these?

Clerk:
Oh, my, yes! It's very, very popular.

Astoria:
Mm. So it's *common,* then.

Clerk:
Common? Well, no. I mean . . . we sell a lot of . . . when I say "a lot" . . . of course, I mean. *All* of our customers are *very* discriminating.

Astoria:
You've got mostly smaller sizes of this blouse. Nothing larger than a size eight, I notice.

Clerk:
Yes, Yes. You're right. Just *perfect* for you.

Astoria:
Seems to suggest that it's the blouse of choice for fat ladies, doesn't it?

Clerk:
Oh, well, no . . . I . . .

Astoria:
Discriminating fat ladies.

Clerk:
Well, we try to have something for . . . we have a wide assortment for *every* taste . . . from petite to . . .

Astoria:
Elephantine.

Clerk:
Full-figured, yes.

Astoria:
I'll take the cream coloured jacket I was looking at earlier and the T'capmin scarf.

Clerk:
Oh, those will look wonderful together.

Astoria:
Once I have the cuffs taken off, a vent added at the back and the cheap wooden buttons replaced with metal ones, I think it will.

Clerk:
Yes. I meant the scarf, though, worn Sepran-style over the jacket like a shawl, with a colourful blouse.

Astoria:
The central design is all right. Once I trim off all the gaudy blue foliage or whatever it is and tuck away the parts where the dyes ran, you won't even notice how asymmetrical it is.

Clerk:
Oh. No. I'm sure you won't.

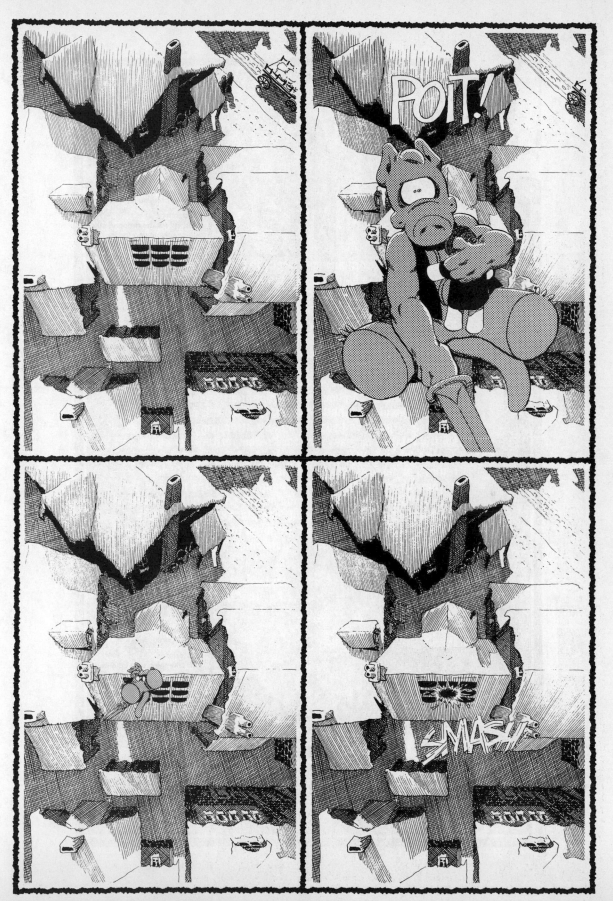

The great flaw of any matriarchy is that it limits political power to those individuals who are the least concerned with progress and achievement. While any society must see the safety of its children as a priority; it must not, should not and can not be that society's first priority. Advancement in the quality of female lives, advancement in the sciences, in medicine, in exploration, in the arts; the conquest of new territories, the expansion of borders in all areas of endeavour, both physical and mental, is critical to the health of empire. An empire which contents itself to build layers of insulation, both physical and mental, around itself and its citizenry, will soon find itself atrophying and falling swiftly into decay; easy prey for its competitors for whom aggression, whether between individuals, geographic regions or empires, stands as the foremost characteristic of their governing body. Where aggression is the primary characteristic of empire, it soon makes short work of those competitors who are quiescent, complacent and passive. The nation-state which is not prepared to consume its neighbours will, inevitably, be consumed by those neighbours.

Astoria
Kevillist Origins

The principle reason that we allow only mothers to govern and to decide the large issues of government in Upper Felda is that they are the only individuals with a genuine stake in the future of our country. If, as many advocate, we extended the voting franchise to daughters once they have reached an arbitrarily chosen age of majority, we would be submitting the fate of our grand and noble experiment to the caprice and whim of individuals who are seeking to escape their own nature. To give them such an outlet would provide an alternative to the following of their True Voice, the dictates of the Goddess Herself and would result in universal madness of the first water. Why have we forbidden men a role in the affairs of state? Because men seek to escape the fact of their expendability (once they have fertilized the egg which becomes new life) with incautious adventurism. Aware that nothing will remain of them to mark their passing, they inevitably seek to make their mark through destruction of peace and order. The young girl's unreasonable fear of childbirth will find outlets in exactly this kind of destructiveness. To open the flood-gates even fractionally; allowing daughters to wield political power; is to invite swift and chaotic inundation.

Cirin
The New Matriarchy

CLAP CLAPCLAPCLAP CLAPCLAPCLAPCL CLAPCLAPCLAPCL LAPCLAPCLAPCLAP PCLAPCLAPCLAP CLAPCLAPCL PCLAP CLAP

OKAY. LET'S GET BACK TO THE *ORIGINAL* QUESTION "DO MOTHERS HAVE A RESPONSIBILITY TO REJECT AN UNSUITABLE SON-IN-LAW"?

YES.

NO.

WHAT DO *YOU* THINK?

MY DAUGHTER MARRIED A MAN WHO LOOKED LIKE A *HYENA*

BUT I KEPT MY MOUTH *SHUT* AND PRETTY SOON ...

BUT DID SHE *LOVE* HIM?

SEE I THINK ...

WELL.

LOVE IS.

LOVE ISN'T THE ANSWER TO EVERYTHING

CLAPCLAP CLAPCLAP CLAPCLAP CLAPCLA LAPCLAPCLAPCLAP CLAPCLAP CLAP LA CLAP AP LA AP

LOVE IS A BIG PART OF IT.

MAYBE THE *BIGGEST* PART OF IT. BUT, YOU KNOW... *REALLY*...

19

NOW WHEN YOU SAY YOU KEPT YOUR MOUTH SHUT...

I NEVER SAID A WORD.

BUT YOU DIDN'T *LIKE* HIM.

I HATED HIM.

CLAPCLAPCLAPCLA
CLAPCLAPCLAPCLAP
CLAPCLAPCLAPCLAP
CLAPCLAPCLAPCLAP

NO ONE WANTS HYENA GRANDCHILDREN

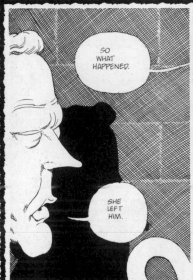

SO WHAT HAPPENED.

SHE LEFT HIM.

CLAPCLAPCLAPCL
LAPCLAPCLAPCLAP
CLAPCLAPCLAPCLA
LAPCLAPCLAPCLAP
CLAPCLAPCLAPCL
LAPCLAP
PCLAP
PCLA
LAP

I JUST THINK WHAT'S *INSIDE* THE PERSON IS MORE IMPORTANT

CLAP
CLAP
CLAP
CLAP

A DONKEY ON THE OUTSIDE IS A DONKEY ON THE *INSIDE*

CLAPCLAPCLAP
CLAPCLAPCLA
LAPCLAPCLAP
CLAPCLAPCLA
PCLAPCLAPCLAP
FCLAPCLAP
APCLAP
PLAP

I'D LIKE TO ASK DR. IRONCAT TO COMMENT HERE...

WHEN WE FEEL HURT OR REJECTED, A LOT OF TIMES WE COVER UP THAT PAIN WITH HOSTILITY TOWARDS SOMEONE WE LOVE VERY MUCH.

I THINK IF MRS GUTCH COULD LOOK AT SOPHIA AND SAY "I LOVE YOU. I UNDERSTAND WHAT YOU'RE GOING THROUGH AND I WANT YOU TO KNOW I'M ON YOUR SIDE BECAUSE I'M YOUR MOTHER AND NO MATTER WHAT I'LL ALWAYS LOVE YOU."

AND IF SOPHIA COULD SAY TO MRS. GUTCH ...

"I KNOW YOU LOVE ME AND I'M SORRY IF MY CHOICES HURT YOU, BUT IT'S MY LIFE AND I HAVE TO LIVE IT MY WAY."

BUT ALSO SAY "HEY, MOM LET'S AGREE TO COMMUNICATE OUR FEELINGS WITHOUT GETTING ANGRY..."

"BECAUSE AFTER ALL IS SAID AND DONE, WE'LL ALWAYS LOVE EACH OTHER AND THAT HAS TO BE MORE IMPORTANT THAN ANY SILLY OLD DISAGREEMENT

DR. IRONCAT IS THE AUTHOR OF "MY MOTHER, MY HUSBAND, MY PAIN"

WE'LL TAKE A SHORT BREAK AND THEN WE'LL BE RIGHT BACK...

CLAPCLAP
CLAPCLAP
LAPCLAP
CLAPCLAP
CLAPCLAP
LAPCLAP
CLAPCLAP
CLAPCLAP

AH HAVE-- AH SAY-- AH HAVE *GOOD NEWS* AND *BAD NEWS*...

TH' *BAD NEWS IS*...

PUNISHEROACH HAS DISAPPEARED!

HELP!

MURDER! THEY KILLED HIM!

HELP!

AH SHIT!

JUST LIKE MOST HOLY!

PANIC!

THE ILLUSIONISTS! THE ILLUSIONISTS!

RUN!!

HELP!!

AN ILLUSION!

NOW WE'RE FUCKED!

RUN AWAY

I TOLD YOU

THE CIRINISTS WILL KILL US ALL!

SAVE US TARIM

IT'S THE WILL OF TARIM

WHAT IS?

WE'RE DOOMED!

WE'RE GOING TO DIE!

RUN

HELP!

DIE!

US BEING FUCKED!

HELP!

TH' *GOOD NEWS* IS; THAT MAKES LITTLE OL' *ME* YO' *NEW* LEADER!

THE ALBINO

IT'S HIS FAULT

STRING 'IM UP

YEAH.

BURN 'IM

KILL 'IM

SENSELESS VIOLENCE.

THAT'LL FIX EVERYTHING.

HEH-HEH. ALL RIGHT.

Y'ALL CAN CARRY ME AROUND ON YOUR SHOULDERS FOR A *LITTLE WHILE*...

BUT *THEN*-- AH SAY *THEN*-- IT'S TIME TO *GIT T' WORK*...

LABOUR INTENSIVE THAT IS...

WELL, ACTUALLY WHEN I SAY THE *FILES* ON ASTORIA ARE MISSING-- I uh...

THE FILE FOLDERS MARKED *"ASTORIA"* ARE ALL THERE BUT THEY... THEY ...DON'T...

THEY DON'T *CONTAIN* INFORMATION ON... ASTORIA

I SEE.

WHAT *DO* THEY CONTAIN?

UM-- THERE WERE *BIRTH CONTROL* PAMPHLETS... *AGRICULTURE MINISTRY* FORECASTS...

SOME uh RECIPES FOR *FUDGE BROWNIES* AND... uh...

uh...

THANK YOU, *CHARISSE*

THAT WILL BE ALL.

YES, GREAT CIRIN...

23

Most of the matriarchy's rhetoric centers on the family (or, rather, the Family); they are obsessive regarding childrens' needs for caring and nurturing and they hold in the greatest contempt those who hold any viewpoint contrary to this. The bond between mother and child is their most sacred totem and their universal rallying cry. It is, therefore, curious to note that at the upper levels of Cirin's government (and, in fact, at most levels of her bureaucracy) the children of her officials are cared for by nannies and governesses until the age of five when they are unceremoniously shipped off to government-run boarding schools. Cirin's own son, Gerrik told me that he did not spend a full day in his mother's company until he was nearly sixteen; and then it was merely to observe her working day so that he might have a fuller appreciation of the complexities of governing Upper Felda.

Astoria
Kevillist Origins

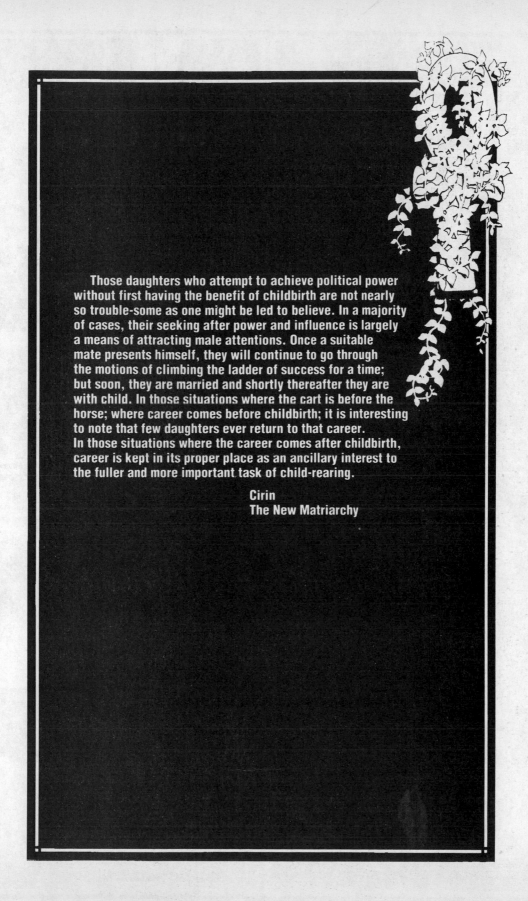

Those daughters who attempt to achieve political power without first having the benefit of childbirth are not nearly so trouble-some as one might be led to believe. In a majority of cases, their seeking after power and influence is largely a means of attracting male attentions. Once a suitable mate presents himself, they will continue to go through the motions of climbing the ladder of success for a time; but soon, they are married and shortly thereafter they are with child. In those situations where the cart is before the horse; where career comes before childbirth; it is interesting to note that few daughters ever return to that career. In those situations where the career comes after childbirth, career is kept in its proper place as an ancillary interest to the fuller and more important task of child-rearing.

Cirin
The New Matriarchy

27

This is Vera, by the way. We've become quite close over the years. She's permanently assigned as my . . . custodian is a nice word for it, I guess. She's supposed to write down everything that I say. I don't think I've said fifty words in five years so her stenographic skills are apt to be a bit rusty. Also, I imagine she's a bit worried as to how long her few wee pads of paper are going to hold out. Add to that the fact that Vera recognizes you and realizes old What's-Her-Name will want to be notified immediately of your . . . return . . . and Vera has herself a real problem. Indeed she does. If she runs to get the guards she'll miss what I have to say to you. If she stays to write down what I tell you, then you get some valuable information old What's-Her-Name would really rather you didn't have.

It's very like a chess game, isn't it, dear? And whichever way Vera turns, she finds herself stalemated; neutralized. Her primary mandate is to write down everything I say and her secondary one is to prevent me from entertaining any visitors. So, the Goddess drops you in through the skylight.

The Goddess is a wonderful chess player.

All women read minds, with very few exceptions.

It's a little more complicated than that. "Woman's intuition" is a nice way of putting it. "Women are more sensitive" is another way of putting it. A not-so-nice way of putting it is that women rape men's minds the way men rape women's bodies. It's not an exact analogy, of course, because rape is invasion and invasion is the man's way, not the woman's way; absorption and consumption are the woman's way; what they're built for. Consider the two genders; one that invades and violates and the other that absorbs and consumes. The nice way of putting it is that they're complementary. The not-so-nice way of putting it is that they deserve each other; serve each other right.

Some women are more efficient at reading minds than are others. Some only pick up impressions; they just get a "feeling" you could say. Others it's as easy as reading a book. For many of them it's like eating a piece of candy; absorbing the entirety of a mind in one gulp.

The matriarchists misinterpret, intentionally I think, the true nature of a woman. They persist in the notion that a woman must adhere to a single male, forming a family unit which they then endeavour to dominate as a superior force. This is nonsensical. The best working model for a woman's life is the beehive; a solitary queen, serviced and catered to by a diverse group of males who exist exclusively to advance her cause. Those with wealth must serve as her personal treasury; those with brawn as her soldier/warriors; those with fertile minds serve as debating adversaries, allowing her to keep sharp her mental skills and to dissect and reinforce her beliefs and theories. The woman who owns the allegiance of the wealthiest, the strongest and the most brilliant of consorts; to her pass the reigns of absolute power. Inevitably she will rise, like heavy cream through thin milk, to the very summit of human existence.

Astoria
Kevillist Origins

A daughter thinks her youth and beauty are timeless. I remember walking through a marketplace with one of my senior advisors and her beautiful daughter (who was then in her mid-teens). A flower-seller extended a single flower to her, with his compliments. This she accepted with only the slightest acknowledgement. My advisor said to her, "You'd better enjoy it while you can. It doesn't last forever, you know." The girl's attentions were drawn elsewhere, to a booth nearby with a display of gaudy trinkets and she ventured no reply. Now in her late twenties, needless to say, the adoring throngs of men who have surrounded her all of her life have dwindled to a handful of low and deceitful characters; charlatans, petty criminals and brigands to a one. Gone are the industrious, reliable and noteworthy suitors of days past. One of these will undoubtedly father her children someday and she will live out her days in degraded circumstances, going from unsuitable mate to unsuitable mate. Her children, when they are of an age to understand, will pity her, mock her, be disgusted by her.

The Goddess has neither mercy upon, nor patience with the willful, the proud and the self-centered woman.

Cirin
The New Matriarchy

Clerk:
Very nice, but of course the drop style earring is for more formal occasions.

Astoria:
Depending on how our discussions turn out, Cirin is either going to accede to my proposals and form a coalition Cirinist/Kevillist government or she's going to throw me back in prison to rot for the rest of my life. Sounds pretty formal to me.

39

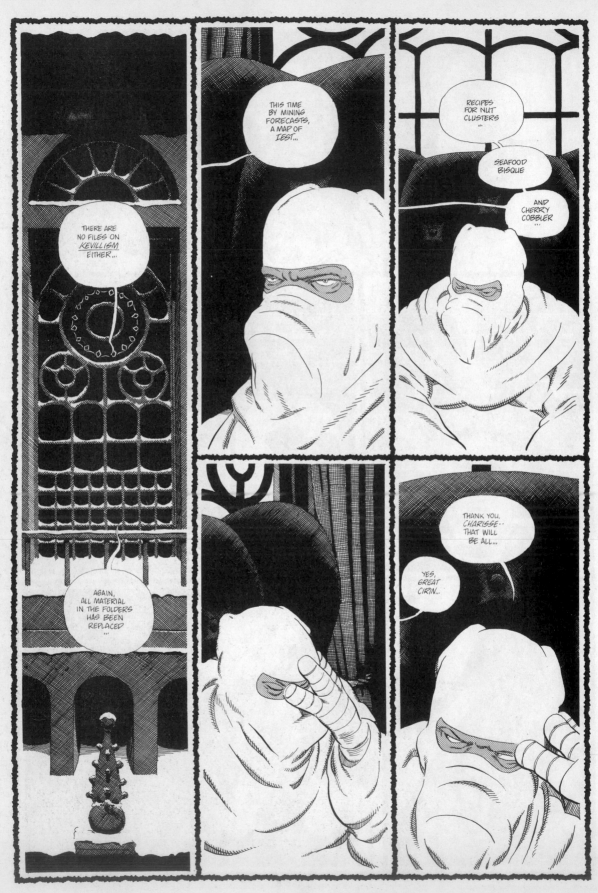

THERE ARE NO FILES ON _KEVILLISM_ EITHER...

AGAIN, ALL MATERIAL IN THE FOLDERS HAS BEEN REPLACED...

THIS TIME BY MINING FORECASTS, A MAP OF _IEST_...

RECIPES FOR NUT CLUSTERS...

SEAFOOD BISQUE

AND CHERRY COBBLER...

THANK YOU, _CHARISSE_-- THAT WILL BE ALL...

YES, GREAT CIRIN...

BENEATH THE RED MARCHES, A NEW PIGTISH ERA BEGINS; WEALTH AND RESOURCES REDISTRIBUTED AMONG ITS POPULACE, NOW ALMOST EXCLUSIVELY COMPOSED OF WIDOWS, CHILDREN, THE AGED AND THE INFIRM. COLOURFUL CLOTHING AND ADORNMENTS ARE EVERYWHERE. EVERY FEW MOMENTS ONE OF THE FEW MALES LEFT BEHIND STAGGERS BY, HIS LIPS STAINED WITH WINE, SURROUNDED BY BEAUTIFUL YOUNG GIRLS. THE AIR IS MADE REDOLENT, BRIEFLY, WITH THE SMELL OF LUST AND SWEAT AND PERFUME. THE SOUND OF LAUGHTER FADES AND CONVERSATION RETURNS TO BABIES, CLOTHING AND THE NOON MEAL.

"Reading" minds isn't the worst of it. The worst of it is changing the minds they absorb; planting contrary thoughts. Changing her mind, the saying goes, is a woman's perogative. Changing *others'* minds is a woman's darkest secret; the black cauldron of which we all partake. Some greedily, some guiltily. Some intentionally, some inadvertently. What's happened in Upper Felda; what is spreading throughout the civilised world; is an abomination. An abomination I was very helpful in bringing about and an abomination which can come to no good end. It is a very large and very dangerous force. Whose minds are being absorbed? Heads of state, business and economic and religious leaders. Whose minds are absorbing them? Unelected wives, grasping and oppor- tunistic mistresses and concubines with handsome eyes and attractive figures. It seemed inconse- quential at the outset, but mind-reading is like any other weapon of power and destruction. It will invariably gravitate to those least suited to wield it and those who are the most unscrupulous about its use. Simply put, the civilised world is being subjected to mental bullying and thuggery on a monumental scale of which it is completely

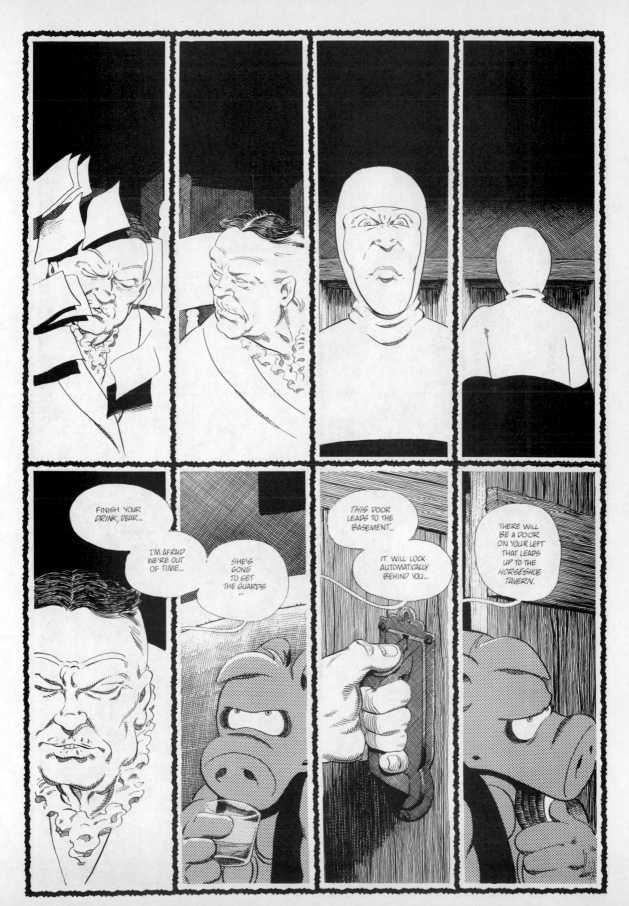

FINISH YOUR DRINK, DEAR...

I'M AFRAID WE'RE OUT OF TIME...

SHE'S GONE TO GET THE GUARDS...

THIS DOOR LEADS TO THE BASEMENT...

IT WILL LOCK AUTOMATICALLY BEHIND YOU...

THERE WILL BE A DOOR ON YOUR LEFT THAT LEADS UP TO THE HORSESHOE TAVERN.

LIKE ALL OTHER TAVERNS, IT'S OFF-LIMITS TO THE CIRINISTS...

"MEN ONLY"

THIS IS ENOUGH MONEY FOR FOOD AND LODGING FOR TONIGHT AND TOMORROW "

I WILL ARRANGE FOR AN ACCOUNT IN YOUR NAME AFTER THAT...

YOU CAN STAY THERE INDEFINITELY IN COMPLETE SAFETY...

HOWEVER, IF YOU TRY TO LEAVE YOU'LL BE ARRESTED ON THE SPOT

THEY'LL BE READY FOR YOU THIS TIME, I'M...

GOODNESS! THEY'RE HERE ALREADY...

BAM BAM BAM

BAM BAM

HURRY ALONG NOW, DEAR "

IT WAS LOVELY TO FINALLY MEET YOU...

CLICK

49

50

FIRST, MY KNOW-IT-ALL-WISE-GUY EVIL TWIN DISAPPEARS

WITHOUT EXPLANATION OR APOLOGY...

NOW, I FIND MYSELF STRIPPED OF MY DIGNIFIED ROBES OF OFFICE; MY HAND-STITCHED PATENT LEATHER SHOES WITH THE CALF-SKIN INSOLES; MY THREE-PIECE CUSTOM-MADE DARK-GRAY-ON-NAVY PIN-STRIPE DOUBLE-BREASTED SUIT WITH HAND-WOVEN GOLD AND BURGUNDY SILK LINING ...

MY GOLD THREAD, CREAM-COLOURED ONE HUNDRED PER CENT (LIGHTLY-STARCHED CUFFS AND COLLAR) COTTON DESIGNER LABEL SHIRT; MY MOTHER-OF-PEARL AND RED GOLD HAND-TOOLED CUFF-LINKS AND MATCHING TIE PIN; MY BLACK SILK AND COTTON BLEND NECK TIE WITH CRUSHED VELVET LINING ...

AGAIN!...

WITHOUT EXPLANATION OR *APOLOGY*...

FAILING THAT WHATEVER MALIGNANT AND UNSEEN FORCE IS AT WORK HERE SHOULD *DEIGN* TO PROFFER AN EXPLANATION

WOULD THAT FORCE AT LEAST OFFER SOME SIGN THAT THESE UNPROVOKED AND UNEXPLAINED ATTACKS UPON MY DIGNITY ARE NOW AT AN *END*?

AM I CORRECT IN INTERPRETING THIS AS A DEFINITE "NO"?

IN THE MIDDLE OF THE FIRST DAY, NOT UNEXPECTEDLY, ONE OF THE REMAINING WARRIORS TAKES UP HIS SWORD AND SEEKS TO RESTORE THE CODES OF MILITARY DISCIPLINE SO FIRMLY INGRAINED IN HIM SINCE INFANCY -- HE IS QUICKLY SURROUNDED BY A CROWD OF WOMEN; EACH INDIVIDUAL BRANDISHING A LONG POLE FITTED WITH A SLIM, TWO-EDGED BLADE WHICH HAS BEEN HONED TO RAZOR SHARPNESS. THEY ARE ABLE TO REMAIN OUTSIDE OF THE SHORT SWORD'S PROXIMITY WHILE SIMULTANEOUSLY INFLICTING GRIEVOUS WOUNDS UPON EXPOSED FLESH. UNABLE TO RETREAT OR ATTACK, THE WARRIOR, IS SOON BATHED IN BLOOD FROM HEAD TO TOE. HE FALLS TO ONE KNEE, THE TRIUMPHANT SHRIEKING LAUGHTER RINGING IN HIS EARS. THEN, EVERYTHING SEEMS TO SLIP AWAY AND HIS CONSCIOUSNESS FADES

JUST ASK FORGIVENESS

CIRIN IS VERY FORGIVING OF *HUMAN* ERROR

YOU COULD BE A GREAT FORCE FOR GOOD.

EVEN NOW.

DO YOU UNDERSTAND WHAT I'M SAYING...?

SHE'S LOST ALREADY

AND SHE KNOWS IT...

AYE?

WHAT WAS THAT?

NOTHING.

JUST THINKING OUT LOUD.

General Greer:
Well, we don't know. We have the transcript from Vera and we know he's in the tavern.

Cirin:
You're certain of that.

General Greer:
Yes. Well, yes and no. We've only observed him in limited interaction with others, so there's a real possibility that he's just an illusion.

General Dworkin:
We have our best-equipped troops stationed there, now, so he can't take us by surprise this time. They're heavily armoured so his sword won't do him much good if he isn't an illusion.

General Greer:
Then there's the doll.

General Dworkin:
Oh, yes. I almost forgot. He's holding a doll, which no one mentioned during the last . . . sighting. A plain rag doll.

Cirin:
A doll.

General Greer:
Yes, we think it might be a provocative gesture on the part of the Illusionists, since it is obviously a maternal symbol. Of course if he's real and he's still a Kevillist, the symbolism is even more significant in that he's holding it in a protective manner and he's already forced one of the tavern residents to pay homage to it.

Cirin:
Homage to a maternal symbol. That doesn't sound like a Kevillist.

General Dworkin:
No, it doesn't; which leads us back to the Illusionists. Someone even suggested that he might have come over to our side.

General Greer:
That's pretty far-fetched.

General Dworkin:
I agree. It's so unexpected and confusing that it would seem to point to Illusionism.

General Greer:
Or Lord Julius. It's the sort of thing he would come up with. Maybe they're still connected in some way.

Cirin:
A maternal symbol. And he's not doing anything?

General Greer:
Just sitting and drinking an ale.

Cirin:
Unbelievable. It must mean something.

General Greer:
Do you want us to go in and get him?

Cirin:
No. The Alcohol Sanction shouldn't be violated. The Illusionists are just trying to provoke us into breaking our own rules so they can use it to fuel an insurgency.

General Greer:
He's murdered a number of mothers, though. Soldiers.

General Dworkin:
He's an illusion. He has to be. If he isn't, how do you explain the doll?

Cirin:
We'll leave him there for the time being. Monitor his conversations. Wait the Illusionists out. They're getting careless. The ascension is at hand. There's no way they can stop it at this point. They're just trying to break our concentration.

General Greer:
Yes. Yes, of course. That must be it.

56

Mrs. Hayes:
Mrs. Thatcher is down there now with Hammond.

Cirin:
It has to be an illusion. Things don't construct themselves like that.

Mrs. Mills:
The designers are beside themselves. You know all of the qualifying they were doing about the purity of the sphere? Ninety percent . . . ninety-five per cent. They aren't qualifying it any more. It makes me suspicious.

Mrs. Hayes:
It's ironic — we kept telling them that they could do it and make it one hundred percent pure and they were the ones who were doubtful. Now they're confident that it can be done and we're the ones with doubts.

Cirin:
We just have to trust that the Goddess is guiding the construction.

Mrs. Hayes:
But if it's the Illusionists — if the expanded forge isn't really there . . .

Mrs. Mills:
It's just a skeleton of wood; one step beyond a blueprint, really. If the principle is sound; and all of the designers and technicians say it is; then it doesn't matter if the skeleton is an illusion. The forge itself will be real.

Mrs. Hayes:
But what if the principle is an illusion? I never understood the mechanics of it in the first place. What would prevent the Illusionists from making the technicians see some miraculous new construction idea that is fundamentally unsound?

Mrs. Mills:
The fact that it's two elements instead of three worries me. First, we needed a mold, a forge and a ladle. Now they're telling us that the ladle is unnecessary. Three elements constitute a queen. Two elements is a priestess.

Cirin:
Unstable.

Mrs. Mills:
It's so Astoria, it squeaks.

Cirin:
You forgot the gold itself. That means it was four elements before; mold, forge, ladle and gold. A king. Now it's three elements; mold, forge and gold.

Mrs. Mills:
Praise the Goddess.

Cirin:
Doubt is going to be our greatest foe as the ascension approaches. We must trust in the Goddess absolutely.

Mrs. Hayes:
Yes, Great Cirin. Of course, you're right.

The Alcohol Sanction is called into question frequently by many sincere followers of our creed. It falls into the same category as prostitution in our view. That which cannot be eliminated must be sequestered. The consumption of alcohol, once isolated from the general community, permits those self-destructive and troublesome elements within the male population to hasten their own demise. Since no one is permitted to leave a licensed establishment until entirely sober, each tavern becomes an effective prison to those unable or unwilling to forego inebriation as a state of perpetual existence. If a husband is absent for three consecutive days owing to intoxication, his marriage is automatically dissolved and his possessions seized and distributed for the general benefit of his own and other needy families. He then becomes a tavern "resident", provided with alcohol and a subsistence diet and mean accommodation for the rest of his days. The average life expectancy of one of these individuals is six to eight months. Indisputably, wives find the enforced separation to be a great trial, but in a majority of cases, they will choose their subsequent life-mate with greater care and less emotion, and will find a reliable provider for themselves and their children.

Cirin
The New Matriarchy

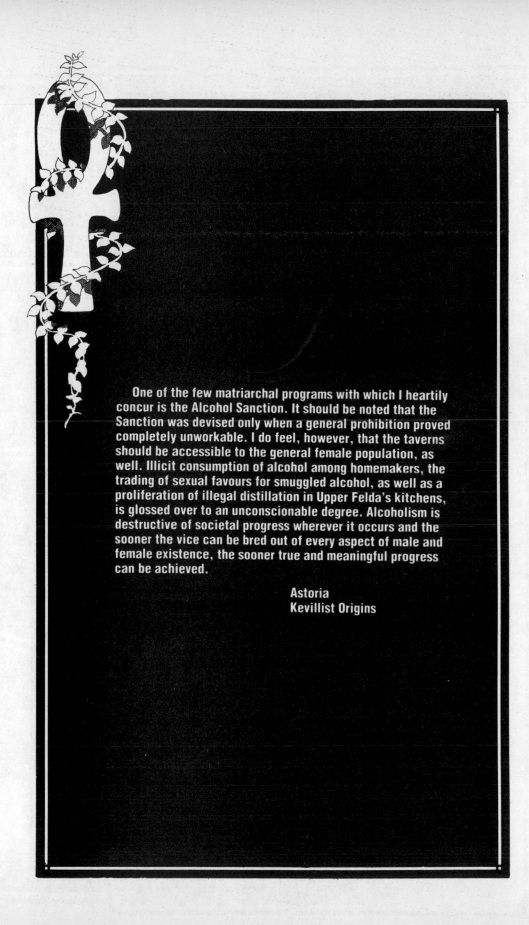

One of the few matriarchal programs with which I heartily concur is the Alcohol Sanction. It should be noted that the Sanction was devised only when a general prohibition proved completely unworkable. I do feel, however, that the taverns should be accessible to the general female population, as well. Illicit consumption of alcohol among homemakers, the trading of sexual favours for smuggled alcohol, as well as a proliferation of illegal distillation in Upper Felda's kitchens, is glossed over to an unconscionable degree. Alcoholism is destructive of societal progress wherever it occurs and the sooner the vice can be bred out of every aspect of male and female existence, the sooner true and meaningful progress can be achieved.

Astoria
Kevillist Origins

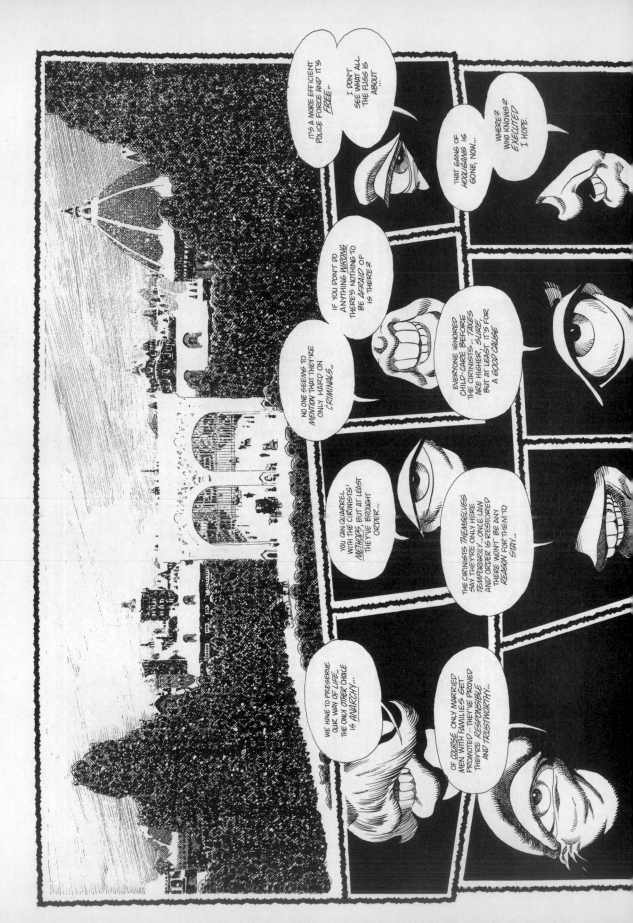

62

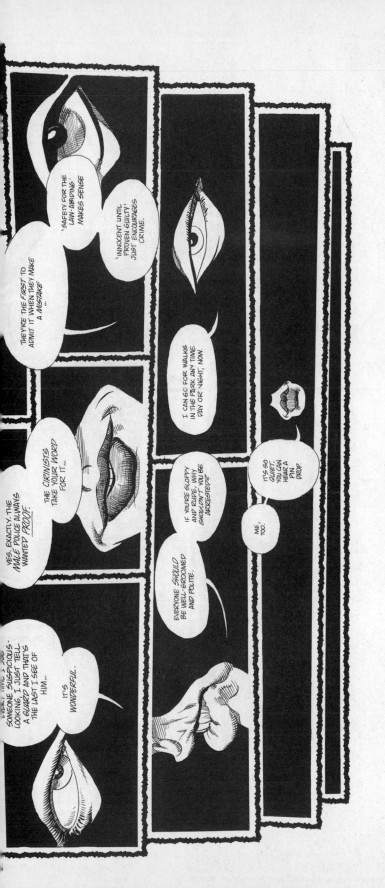

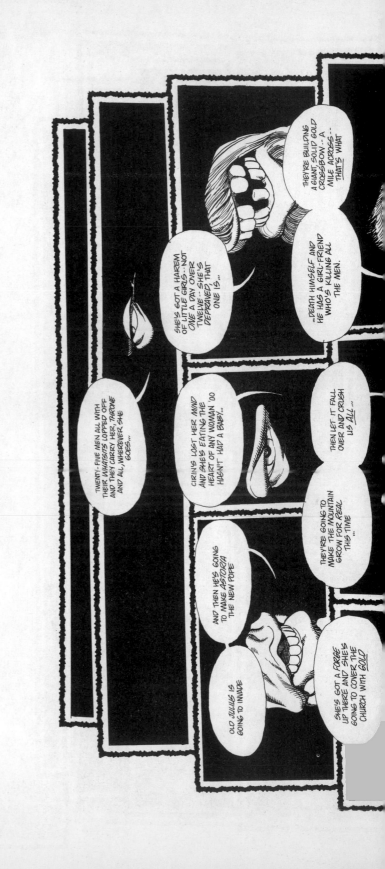

General Greer:
First, the signs have been changed from "Roachland" to "Swoon Country". Again, we have no idea what that means.

General Dworkin:
We've been able to scan nothing of Skull man. As per our discussions late last night, we decided to send in a reconnaissance group over the rooftops. There's a young woman who seems to have the same kind of weapons that Skull man used on the first assault team.

Cirin:
A woman?

General Dworkin:
Yes. Very young; wearing the sacred symbol. Dressed entirely in black. We tried to monitor her thoughts and drew a blank.

Cirin:
She's screening, then?

General Dworkin:
Evidently.

Cirin:
Kevillist?

General Dworkin:
That would be our best guess. We have no idea how she knew our people were on the roof, but she took them all out with pinpoint accuracy. Twenty dead.

Cirin:
Dead are confirmed?

General Greer:
Yes. No chance of it being an illusion.

General Dworkin:
She has a companion. A large man in black robes. Both are described as extremely paleskinned. We haven't been able to scan him either. Except for one word. "Blossom".

Cirin:
Sounds like an ascension reference.

General Greer:
Blossom. Exactly.

General Dworkin:
I'd like to recommend an all-out assault, but at this point it would be highly inadvisable. First, we don't know where Skull man is hiding and we have to assume he's still there and fully armed. And we have no idea at this point who else is down there.

Cirin:
So your recommendation is . . .?

General Dworkin:
Hold the perimeter as we've been doing, but bring in some cross-bows and make it a little more secure; sand-bags, pike and what-not. We're still not letting anyone in, but we'd like to make sure that they don't break out of the confined area.

Cirin:
Yes. Immediately.
Good thinking.

70

72

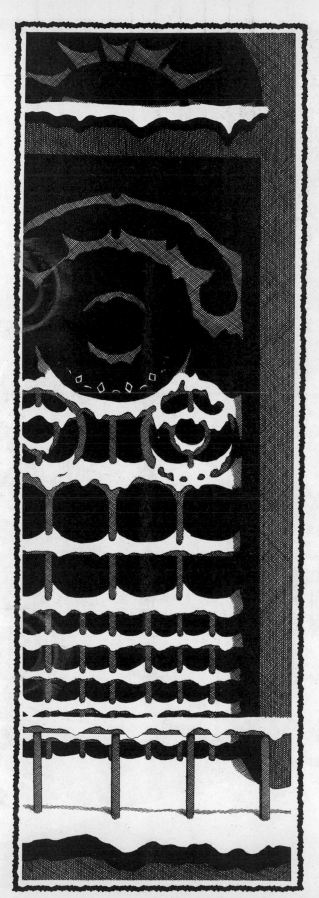

General Greer:
Great Cirin, I think
. . . I strongly
recommend that
we go in.

Cirin:
And if he's just
standing on the
steps up to the
second floor?
Or if he was just
an illusion?

General Greer:
I just don't think
we can afford the
risk. If we can't see
him . . .

Cirin:
A few dozen
armoured soldiers
breaking into a
quiet little tavern
in a quiet little
neighbourhood?
You'd make us a
laughing-stock . . .

General Greer:
But if he's . . . if
he's actually the . . .
if he's the one that
they've all been . . .
waiting for . . .

Cirin:
A folk tale. A lower
City folk tale and
that's going to be
your reason to
violate the Alcohol
Sanction. I thought
you had a little
more back-bone
than that, General.

General Greer:
I'm not saying that
he is. Far from it.
But if they believe
that he is. I don't
really see how we
can . . . I think the
risk . . .

Cirin:
I think we are all
going to be better
served by con-
centrating on the
True Ascension
and remaining
calm. Panicking
over a folk tale is
hardly going to
assist us in that,
is it, General.

General Greer:
Great Cirin, I just
mean to . . .

Cirin:
Is. It.

General Greer:
No, Great Cirin. I'm
sorry. You're right,
of course. Praise
the Goddess.

Cirin:
I'm going to say
this to all of you,
and I am only
going to say it
once. This panic
has got to stop.
This panic *will*
stop. He is not
behaving in any
manner that we
might have
anticipated. That
only increases the
likelihood that he
is an illusion; pure
and simple. Do
you understand
me? You are to
maintain observa-
tion. There is
nothing compli-
cated or difficult
about that order,
now is there? If he
starts making a
speech, you are
authorized to go
in. Nothing too
complicated or
difficult about that,
either, is there?
We are nearing the
day of the Final
Ascension.
Everything is
running very, very
smoothly. You are
Soldiers of the
Goddess. I expect
you to behave as
such. If I become
aware of any one
of you behaving
like some weak,
snivelling . . .

General Greer:
Great Cirin.

Cirin:
How dare you
interrupt me. That
is exactly the sort
of . . .

General Greer:
Great Cirin, look
outside.

Cirin:
It's raining. Yes.
By the Goddess
are you now afraid
of a little . . .

General Greer:
The Tower,
Great Cirin.

Cirin:
The Tower?
What about
the . . .

Cirin:
Oh. Oh my.

In the history of Iest, there have been several attempts, some real, some illusory, at an ascension into heaven. In each case, the individual attempting that ascension has been male. In each case, the Tower has risen erratically, and has been structurally unsound. In each case, it has then collapsed on the Lower City, causing massive destruction, nearly unimaginable loss of life and injury. This, then, is the surest sign that exists of the Goddess' intolerance of male-dominated, male-directed society. It will be a mother who ascends, when the time comes. And that time will be soon. The Goddess will reach down to us, even as we reach up to Her. When that glorious connection is made; when that wondrous day arrives; the long-promised Golden Age will dawn and our successes and triumphs in Upper Felda will pale by comparison; mere flint, mere stone, mere spark, beside the miraculous, world-wide Blaze of Glory that is yet-to-be.

Cirin
The New Matriarchy

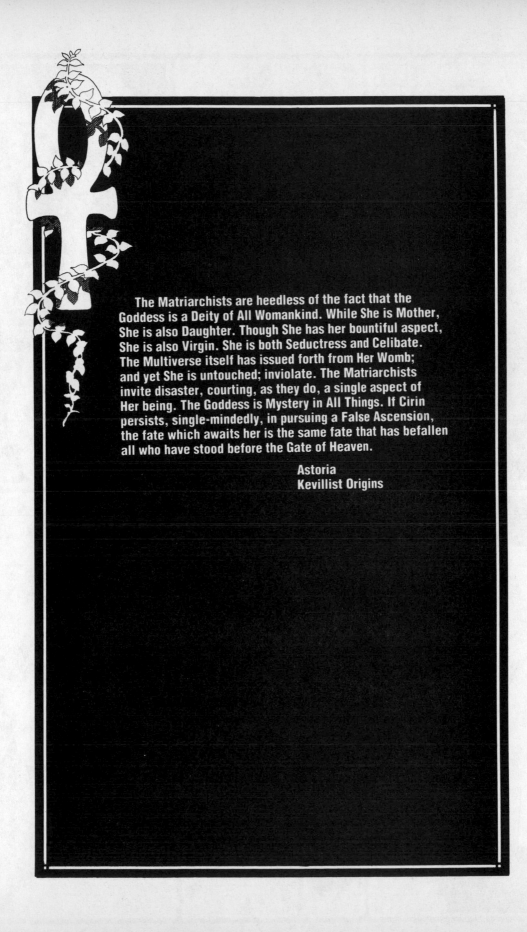

The Matriarchists are heedless of the fact that the Goddess is a Deity of All Womankind. While She is Mother, She is also Daughter. Though She has her bountiful aspect, She is also Virgin. She is both Seductress and Celibate. The Multiverse itself has issued forth from Her Womb; and yet She is untouched; inviolate. The Matriarchists invite disaster, courting, as they do, a single aspect of Her being. The Goddess is Mystery in All Things. If Cirin persists, single-mindedly, in pursuing a False Ascension, the fate which awaits her is the same fate that has befallen all who have stood before the Gate of Heaven.

Astoria
Kevillist Origins

80

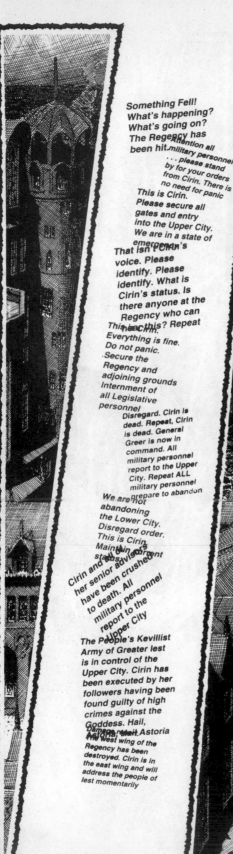

Something Fell!
What's happening?
What's going on?
The Regency has been hit.

Attention all military personnel ... please stand by for your orders from Cirin. There is no need for panic

This is Cirin. Please secure all gates and entry into the Upper City. We are in a state of emergency.

That isn't Cirin's voice. Please identify. Please identify. What is Cirin's status. Is there anyone at the Regency who can hear this? Repeat

This is Cirin. Everything is fine. Do not panic. Secure the Regency and adjoining grounds Internment of all Legislative personnel

Disregard. Cirin is dead. Repeat, Cirin is dead. General Greer is now in command. All military personnel report to the Upper City. Repeat ALL military personnel prepare to abandon

We are not abandoning the Lower City. Disregard order. This is Cirin. Maintain current status.

Cirin and her senior advisors have been crushed to death. All military personnel report to the Upper City

The People's Kevillist Army of Greater lest is in control of the Upper City. Cirin has been executed by her followers having been found guilty of high crimes against the Goddess. Hail, Astoria

Damage report. The West wing of the Regency has been destroyed. Cirin is in the east wing and will address the people of lest momentarily

Quiet meditation is required in a crisis period. Cirin offers her reassurances to all mothers

Your babies are dying. The babies are dying because of the false mother. Open yourself to the real crisis. The babies are dying.

Stop. Stop listening. It's all lies. All lies. Hear not the false voices of the wicked mothers. They have brought this disaster upon

This is Cirin. We are not worthy Cirin has been slightly injured. Repeat slightly injured. She is being transferred to a safe location in the Upper City and will address the People of lest session on her arrival

...weapons by mothers is strictly forbidden during a crisis period. Please surrender all weapons to local authorities

Something fell. The false mother has been destroyed. All hail Astoria

Please make note of all traitors. Execution has been authorized. Repeat Cirin's order all... The Regency is now under the direct command the Kevillist People's A Astoria draws to her ascension. The security mothers and children will be guaranteed. Join us.

We are a... Our women poisoned... belief. We... undone... an execution... Execution... false People... has been... by Gene... by the nam... Living... Strike... Cirin

Lies. They're all lies. The babies are dying. The babies are dying. We're killing them. Why are they not spared? The blood of innocents is on our hands

And he ⋯ lay waste to the false temples. The True Church endures. The Regency was false and is destroyed. Praise the Goddess.

Be at peace. Be at peace. We are all one. We are of the Goddess and she is of us

Cirin is safe and joins with Astoria in asking for calm. Please remain calm and all will be made clear to those who follow all aspects of the Living Goddess.

Throw down your weapons Seek her mercy Seek salvation Seek the Goddess

Lower City is safe. The Goddess has disfavour only for the Upper City. See the sign now. See what the false mothers have brought upon themselves

Everyone in the Upper City is dead. Everyone. Flee the Upper City and save yourselves

HALT!

I HAVE ORDERS TO TAKE THIS *PRISONER* TO CIRIN AT THE *REGENCY* ...

IT'S ASTORIA OVER HERE

ASTORIA LOOK ASTORIA

QUICK

ASTORIA

EXECUTE HER

HER

"IT'S ASTORIA HAIL

HAIL ASTORIA

HER!

ASTORIA

KILL! HER! GET HER NOW!

GET BACK! GET BACK!

THE ROAD TO THE REGENCY IS *CLOSED.*

WE'LL JUST HAVE TO TAKE THE LONG WAY AROUND, THEN.

IT'S ASTORIA! HAIL ASTORIA!

WCK

GET HER OUT HERE!

KILL HER!!

GET BACK

89

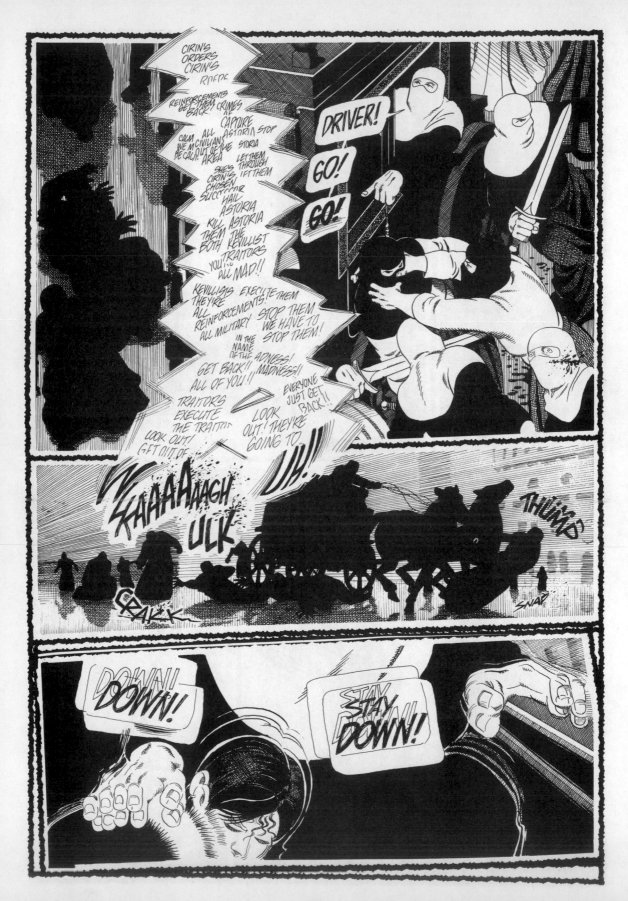

92

RUN! RUN!

SHIELD YOUR THOUGHTS
"

LISTEN
...

WHAT.

I REALLY HATE TO MAKE THINGS COMPLICATED FOR YOU
...

BUT I'M AFRAID I'M ABOUT

TO

I'M THE *LAST RULER* OF A *DYIN' RACE!*

...

AH DON'T ~~HAVE~~ ANY FAMILY!

Nonsense, my sister

...

Think back.

...

Remember.

We have many names ...

... in many ... realities

We are ...

"The Clueless"

...

When the Multiverse was born ...

We were mere infants.

The Matriarchists are at great pains to eliminate the true histories of female dominated societies. Most particularly they disavow any awareness of the brief period in the history of Iest's Upper City when the singular philosophies of the T'capmin writer Kevil took hold. To me, this was the only period of enlightenment in the sordid history of Cirinism when a natural division of responsibility and interests was put in place; Mothers in charge of all issues governing the family and child care and Daughters in charge of all issues not concerned with family and child care. The evolution from one group to the other was natural and well-suited to the needs of society as a whole. Upon giving birth, a woman's tasks changed from those extroverted concerns to a mother's more naturally introverted concerns. The fact that the matriarchy, as constituted in Upper Felda, has been forced to become totalitarian and dictatorial is the surest sign that it is completely out of synch with the natural rhythms of human existence.

Astoria
Kevillist Origins

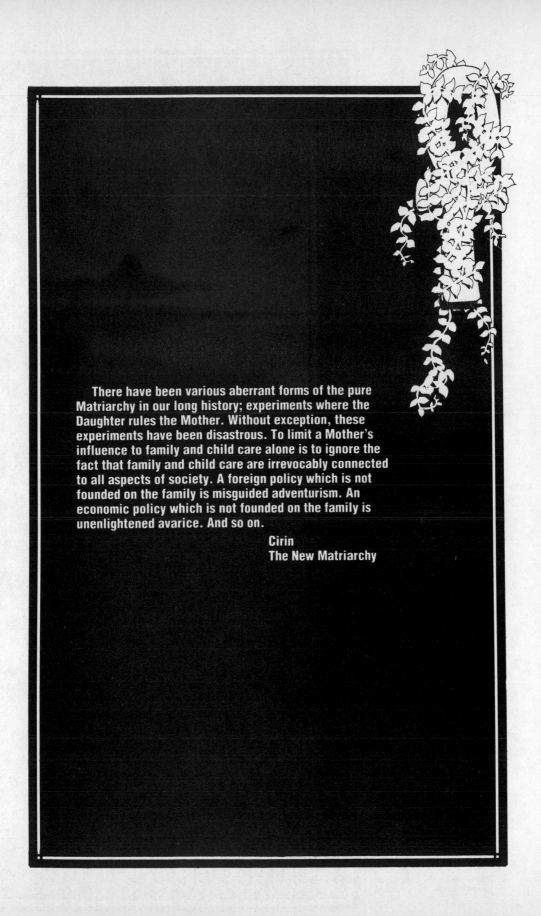

There have been various aberrant forms of the pure Matriarchy in our long history; experiments where the Daughter rules the Mother. Without exception, these experiments have been disastrous. To limit a Mother's influence to family and child care alone is to ignore the fact that family and child care are irrevocably connected to all aspects of society. A foreign policy which is not founded on the family is misguided adventurism. An economic policy which is not founded on the family is unenlightened avarice. And so on.

Cirin
The New Matriarchy

See, *I* was trying to find *her* and *she* was trying *not* to let me find her and then I got scared. I had this really strong feeling that something really really *bad* was going to happen. I kept thinking, "Cerebus is going to kill me — why is Cerebus going to kill me?"

But . . .

And then the mountain fell over and suddenly she was right there! Right there in front of me!

The fake Regency Elf.

No, dopey pants; the *real* one. *I* 'm the *fake!*

But . . .

See, she was the legend; the one everyone had known about for years and years and *years*. But she doesn't look like me a *bit*. She has dark wavy hair and big slanted eyes and tall pointy ears and she looks like a porcelain *doll* !

But . . .

See, *she* couldn't exist outside of the Ambassador Suite. That's how I knew she was the real one. I could go outside and play wickets or visit the kitchen or go to the lobby but when the Ambassador Suite got smunched she just went away poof!

Uh . . . so where did you come from?

I came from *you*, silly-silly, I already *told* you that!

No you didn't.

Yes I did.
Oh, no. Wait.
That's right.
I didn't.

Well, I did! I came from you.

100

See, you were *in* the Ambassador Suite the first time you went to the Suenteus Po Place and you were zooming and zipping and swooping and veering and zigging and zagging and swooshing and swishing and . . .

Cerebus gets the idea.

So with all that zooming and zipping and . . . us . . . and that stuff and the REAL Regency Elf being right there, see, that made me. See?

Huh.

HEY! I JUST REALIZED!

Realized what?

I'm your DAUGHTER!

WHAT!?

I'm your DAUGHTER!

THAT'S THE CRAZIEST THING CEREBUS EVER HEARD!

It's NOT crazy. I'm your DAUGHTER! Your DREAM DAUGHTER! I look like the girl you lived next door to when you were growing up and I look like Jaka and I look like Katrina and I look like Doris and . . .

YOU ARE NOT CEREBUS' DAUGHTER!

Yes I am! Yes I am!

YOU ARE NOT!

Am too! Am too! And I can prove it!

Yeah? How?

Make love to me!

ELF! WHAT A THING TO SAY!

See? See?

You wanted to make love to the girl next door!

Yes, but . . .

And you wanted to make love to Katrina!

Yes, but . . .

And you DID make love to Jaka!

Yes, but . . .

C'mon, what are you waiting for?

Look, I'll take off my dress.

ELF! DON'T YOU DARE! STOP IT! STOP THAT NOW! STOP THIS FOOLISH-NESS RIGHT NOW YOUNG LADY OR CEREBUS WILL . . . WILL . . .

HA!
I'm yo-ur
daugh-ter!

I'm yo-ur
daugh-ter!

**This is a
dream.
Of course.
This is too
weird. It's a
dream.**

Uh uh.

**Sure. It's a
dream and
Cerebus
is going
to wake
up and
Cerebus
will go and
get himself
a nice
drink.**

Uh uh.
It's LIKE a
dream, but
it's different.
You're really
here.

**No no.
Cerebus
is just
dreaming
and when
Cerebus
wakes up,
Cerebus
will get
himself a
nice drink
and . . .**

What do
you want
to drink,
Daddy?

**An ale . . .
a nice tall
. . . DON'T
DO THAT!**

Don't do
what?

**DON'T
CALL
CEREBUS
. . .**

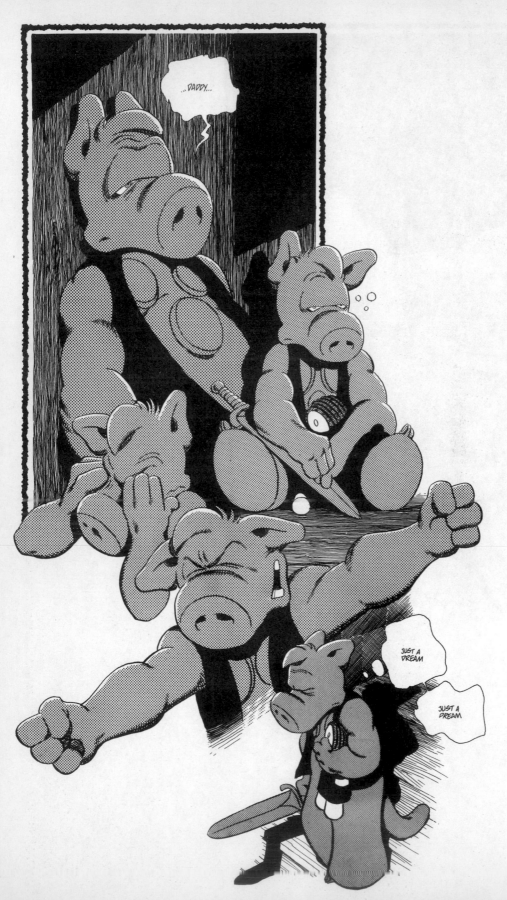

105

ALE.

AH JEST FOUND OUT IT AIN'T NO RUMOUR!

A WHOMPIN' BIG HUNK O' TH' MOUNTAIN A-FELL ON TH' UPPER CITY AT HAGH NOON T'DAY!!

AN' SMASHED TH' REGENCY HO-TELL TUH SMITHEREENIES

... AND A SMALL BUCKET OF SCOTCH.

YES, SOR, MEESTER CEREBOOS THE PUP!

RIGHT AWAY.

DEGENERATE

AH!

YOU'RE AWAKE.

GREAT ASTORIA.

WE AWAIT YOUR INSTRUCTIONS

OH GOOD.

I MANAGED TO WAKE UP ON THE RIGHT TEAM.

WHO'S WINNING?

WE HAVE MANY UNCONFIRMED REPORTS OF CIRIN'S DEATH

THE CIRINISTS, AS A RESULT, ARE IN COMPLETE DISARRAY ''

OH REALLY.

AND WHAT-- THEORETICALLY-- DID SHE DIE *OF*.

A LARGE SPIRE GREW ON THE MOUNTAIN

WHEN IT BROKE OFF AND FELL OVER ...

IT CRUSHED THE REGENCY HOTEL...

THE *UPPER* CITY...

CURIOUS.

HOW *SECURE* ARE WE HERE?

WE HAVE HEAVILY- ARMED GUARDS STATIONED AT EVERY ENTRANCE... THE CIRIN LOYALISTS ARE KEEPING THEIR DISTANCE...

THERE ARE A NUMBER OF SUPPORTERS AND CURIOSITY-SEEKERS MILLING AROUND THE GROUNDS...

NOTHING WE CAN'T HANDLE

TO BE HONEST, EVERYONE IS JUST ... STUNNED WOULD BE THE BEST WORD FOR IT ...

JUST GOING THROUGH THE *MOTIONS* ... WAITING TO SEE WHAT HAPPENS *NEXT*...

I'LL BET.

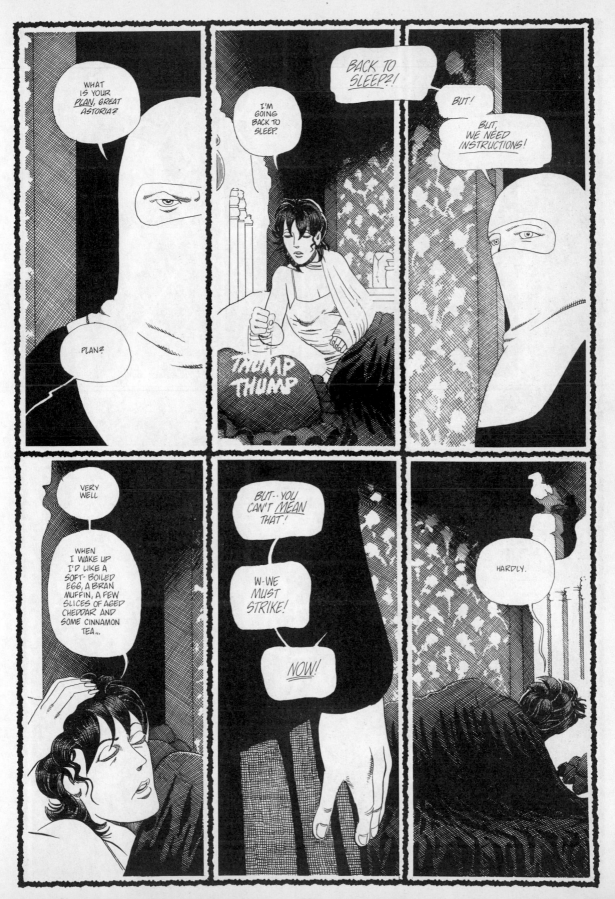

SO THEN, CEREBUS DOVE BACK INSIDE THE TOWER WHERE THE BIG MAN AND WOMAN APOCALYPSE BEAST COULDN'T GET HIM

AND THE TOWER WAS STILL GETTING TALLER AND TALLER, BUT IT WAS *ALSO* GETTING NARROWER AND NARROWER, SEE?

SO THEN CEREBUS CAN HEAR THE TOWER STARTING TO MAKE THIS *CRACKING* NOISE AND BEFORE YOU KNOW IT

Y'KNOW-- AH HED ME A DREAM JEST LAK THET ONCE...

THAR WUZ THIS BIG OL' HAIRY BLUE DAWG...

IT WASN'T A **DREAM**, YOU MORON!

CEREBUS ASCENDED INTO VANAHEIM!

I THUTT Y'U SET Y'U LENTET UN THE *MUUN*...

YEAH -- THET'S RAGHT

THET'S WHUT YUH SED.

On the subject of dreams, most particularly, the matriarchists reveal themselves to be dictatorial and uncompromising. From a very early age, they train their daughters to regard all of existence as real and tangible; that any transgression awake or asleep is to be regarded as equally suspect and as a punishable offence. Naturally enough, there is no way to control people's dreams, but their vehemence on the subject has caused more than one small child to regard herself as depraved, evil and unworthy through having dreamt herself in a circumstance which does not meet with matriarchal approval. Dreamers, awake and asleep, have been responsible for most, if not all, of the great developments in all areas of human endeavour. Small wonder that, apart from inventing itself, the matriarchy is barren of anything that could (even by the most charitable) be described as an idea; and further that they are always in the forefront of those who seek to oppress, inhibit and eradicate new thought. Until, of course, that new thought proves itself beneficial to their society, whereupon they embrace it whole-heartedly and strike all reference to their original opposition from any written record.

Astoria
Kevillist Origins

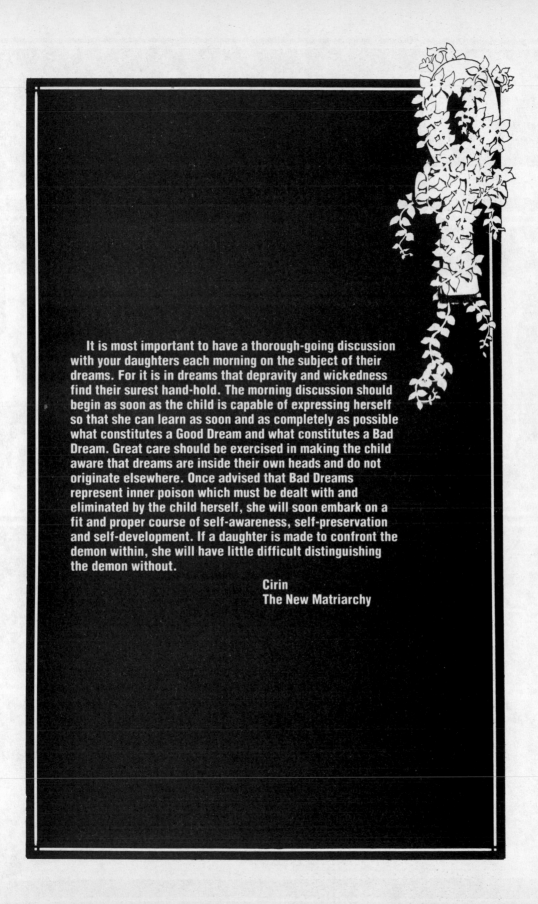

It is most important to have a thorough-going discussion with your daughters each morning on the subject of their dreams. For it is in dreams that depravity and wickedness find their surest hand-hold. The morning discussion should begin as soon as the child is capable of expressing herself so that she can learn as soon and as completely as possible what constitutes a Good Dream and what constitutes a Bad Dream. Great care should be exercised in making the child aware that dreams are inside their own heads and do not originate elsewhere. Once advised that Bad Dreams represent inner poison which must be dealt with and eliminated by the child herself, she will soon embark on a fit and proper course of self-awareness, self-preservation and self-development. If a daughter is made to confront the demon within, she will have little difficult distinguishing the demon without.

Cirin
The New Matriarchy

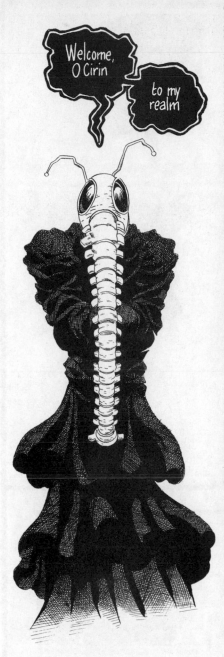

General Greer:
We have to face facts. Any time we try to announce anything or reassure the public, it just starts another cacaphony. We have loyal supporters who have secured the grounds of the Papal Residence. Astoria's supporters have secured a small hotel at the edge of the disaster site. Astoria hasn't said . . .

General Dworkin:
I say we just storm the damn hotel and execute her.

General Greer:
You keep saying that, and I keep trying to explain to you that no one is listening to us. They all know when it's Cirin in their heads, but they don't know us from Eve. No one is going to launch an attack with a hundred different voices saying they're us and telling them to do a hundred different things. We've . . .

General Steinem:
I think you're missing the point, whether anyone listens to us or not. We don't know what Cirin wants us to do. Her last command was to bring Astoria to her for questioning. If Astoria dies in an assault we can't magically bring her back to life and if we bring her in alive . . . what are we going to do? Bring her in here and tell her to wait for Cirin to regain consciousness? She'll just declare herself the new Cirin and who can say which way that will go? She still has a good case for being the Western Pontiff. You bring her into the heart of the Eastern Church and you might as well have united the two . . .

General Dworkin:
Who said anything about bringing her in here? We take her to a cell and hold her until Cirin comes to.

General Greer:
You've got fifteen miles of sacred road between that hotel and the church. Some illusionist conjures up a lady in white robes over the carriage and we're not going to get her past the Treasury building without a full-scale uprising. She's got a handful of followers over there now. Let them make the first move. We have two legions in a ring around the hotel. It's no different from Roachland . . .

General Steinem:
Swoon Country.

General Greer:
Whatever. Or Cerebus. Cirin's pattern has been pretty obvious. She told us to anticipate little pockets of 'infection' with the Ascension at hand. In each case, her orders were the same: a strong military presence around the perimeter. No one in. No one out. Containment, pure and simple.

General Greer:
I think you can understand that with so much at stake, we need more information on her condition. Specifics.

Dr. Cameron:
I understand that. The specifics haven't changed since I examined her earlier today. She has a minor fracture of one of the bones in her right forearm. I've put a cast on and the fracture should be healed in eight to ten weeks. She has a minor fever. Her respiration is normal. Her pulse is normal.

General Greer:
And she's in a coma.

Dr. Cameron:
Well. I haven't changed my opinion on that either. A coma is brought on by three things; disease, injury or poison. She shows no symptoms of any disease with which I'm familiar, although since she can't answer any questions, all I can do is go by appearances as well as examining any bodily excretions, which have showed no abnormalities. You've provided me with samples of all the food and drink that she's consumed in the last two days and there's no sign of any poison. And apart from the fracture in her arm and some minor bruising on her shoulders and upper body from the rubble that fell on her, there's no sign of injury. Her pupils respond normally to strong light.

General Greer:
So you still think that she's . . .

Dr. Cameron:
Asleep. Yes.

General Greer:
Then why doesn't she wake up?

Dr. Cameron:
That I couldn't tell you. I've discussed this with a number of other physicians, I've referred to all texts available on the subject and I'm unable to find anything which is applicable. The world of medicine is filled with the unexplainable. We know a great deal more now than we knew ten years ago, but medical conditions that we don't recognize are not unusual. When they occur, all we can do is observe the condition and make notes on it.

General Greer:
And what happens in these unrecognizable cases?

Dr. Cameron:
The patient gets better or the patient dies.

General Greer:
Is it sorcery, then?

Dr. Cameron:
My personal opinion? As a physician I believe that unexplained conditions get blamed on sorcery because our knowledge of medicine is limited. I think when the day comes that we know all there is to know about the human body, the very idea of sorcery will vanish into the realm of folklore.

General Greer:
The soldier who brought you here will return you to your home. You will be summoned to conduct another examination around dawn.

Dr. Cameron:
Certainly. Good evening.

General Steinem:
Well, why not bring in a witch or a healer of some kind?

General Greer:
Consider the likelihood that they are Illusionists. Most of them are you know. Do you know enough about it to choose the right one?

General Steinem:
Well, you've brought in that Doctor. I don't really see that there's a great deal of difference. Most of *them* are Kevillists. How do *you* know that *you* chose the right one?

General Greer:
Dr. Cameron has provided invaluable assistance to Cirin in her development of many of the potions and medications that save hundreds and hundreds of . . .

General Dworkin:
Maybe *he* poisoned her. Have you considered that? Swabbing those pads around in her mouth and her nostrils and her ears and her . . . her . . .

General Greer:
He said that bodily excretions are the only things that he has to . . .

General Dworkin:
It's unnatural, is all. Unnatural and disrespectful. The living incarnation of the Goddess is in our care and we stand around with our mouths open while some pervert goes poking and prodding around under her night-shirt as if she were some sort of . . .

General Steinem:
I agree. So much of this is starting to seem like a judgement on us all. The mountain crushes the Upper City for the first time in history and then we allow ourselves to be a party to the violation of the Living Goddess. I think we've earned her disfavour for becoming as corrupt as Astoria herself. The Goddess is testing our purity and I say we've failed Her.

General Greer:
This is no time for some hysterical . . .

General Dworkin:
Haven't you noticed the smell in here? We've brought corruption on ourselves. We've become a party to it. A catalyst for it. Everything we do just drags us deeper and deeper into the cesspool Cirin has always warned us about. What are we going to do? Answer me that. *What* are we going to *do*?

General Greer:
The only thing we *can* do. Wait for Cirin to awaken.

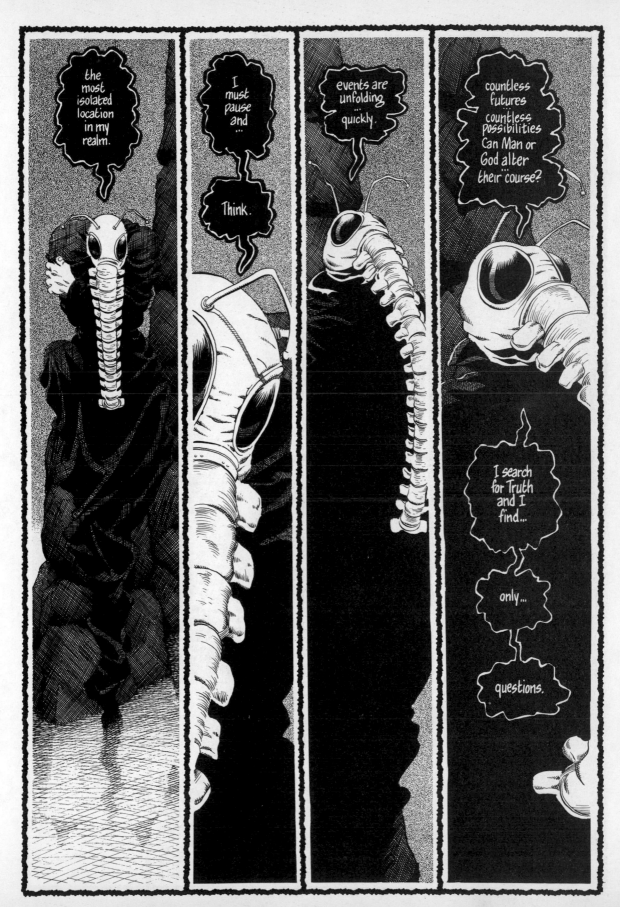

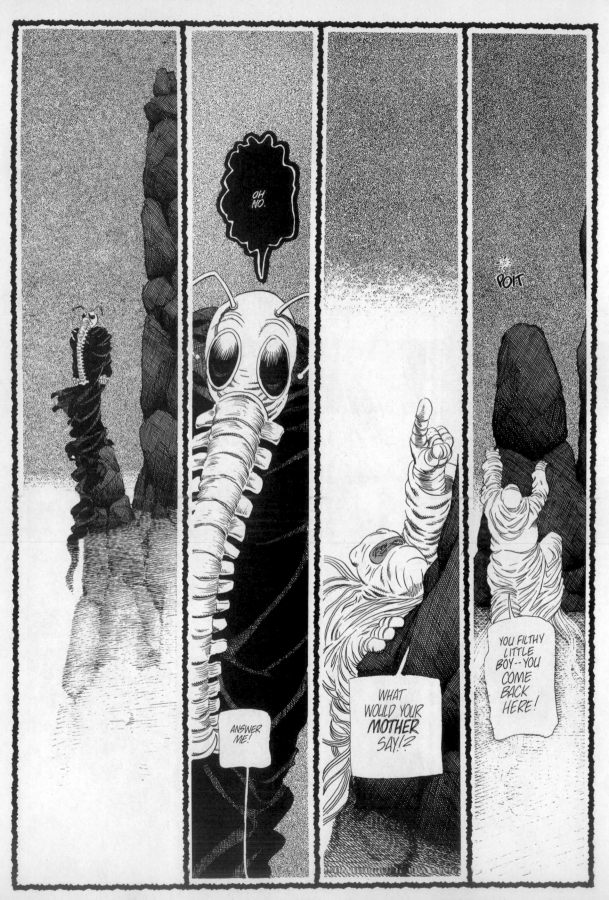

126

ND THEN JAKA understood. The maze and the book and her life were all connected.

Each baffle in the maze had been another chapter in the book; another episode in her life. It was dancing that moved her forward. When dancing was the center of her life she made progress through the maze. When dancing was not the center of her life, she would re-read the same paragraph a dozen times without comprehension. The maze would close itself off, becoming a small and confining cell with hedges for walls and try as she might she would be unable to find an exit. Then, just as suddenly, her mind would cease its wandering and she would be caught up in the story unfolding before her, unaware that she had turned a page or finished a chapter. Within the maze, an opening would appear and she would find the seemingly-endless passages were suddenly as familiar to her as the back of her own hand. Now, she was nearing her destination, the center of the maze. She turned right and then left and then right again. In a moment's time, she had stepped into a wide and quiet clearing. At its center was an ornate stone chair, intricately carved. On the back of the chair were four white candles, burning brightly and filling the air with the pleasing scent of blossoms in spring-time. On the seat itself there was a book. She picked it up and traced the gilt lettering on the front with her finger-tip. 'Jaka's Story', it said. She opened the cover and began to read.

IF I CAN DO IT, YOU CAN, the book began. The first page described the maze in such vivid terms that she could see it before her eyes, as if she were a bird flying above it. While she had so often felt that the hedges grew and that the passageways went from wide to narrow, she could see now that the height of the hedges and the width of the passageways were uniform and symmetrical.

She was aware that a small girl had stepped forward into the clearing and she felt, then, a pang of anxiety. She didn't wish to stop reading. But, if the child spoke to her, she would have to answer out of politeness. Even as she thought this, however, the child dropped lightly onto the carefully-groomed carpet of grass and began speaking in a low voice to her doll.

You see, Missy, the child was saying, things really don't change at all. It's just that when you're afraid or when you're angry or when you're sad, you can't see that *you're* the one who changed; not everyone and everything else.

Jaka could feel that the child was very much at peace being by herself, with only her little doll for company.

If I can do it, you can.

It was the way the story began and the way that the story ended.

Even as Jaka marvelled at the simple, yet inviolable balance of the book, life and maze, she sensed that the little girl was now standing beside her, looking up at her with wide and compassionate eyes.

Cerebus is alive, you know, she whispered.

And he loves you very much.

132

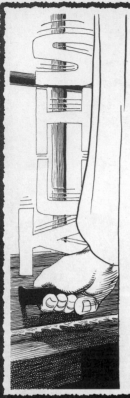

134

...THAT YOU PROPOSE TO UNITE TWO *MALE* CHURCHES?

...THAT YOU *DELUDE* YOURSELF THAT YOU CAN TAKE THEIR...*TRANSGRESSIONS* UNTO YOUR *BOSOM?*

THAT SOME MANNER OF... *REDEMPTION* WILL ENSUE?

THAT YOUR BLIND DESIRE FOR *POWER* HAS...

I *SAID* ...

SHUT UP!!

WHAT WOULD YOUR *MOTHER* SAY, ASTORIA ?

ABOUT USING YOUR *FISTS* TO SETTLE YOUR...

SHUT!

UP!

General Steinem:
Look! Look at that.
Another welt. He just
walked into the room
and another welt
appears on her face.

Dr. Cameron:
Please let me
examine her.
If you'll just . . .

General Dworkin:
Examine her?
It's your
examinations that've
led to this. What have
you done to her?

General Greer:
Please.
There can't be any
harm in this . . .

General Steinem:
I think you've
said quite
enough already.
This is sorcery.
Open your eyes.

General Dworkin:
Yes. Sorcery.
Dr. Cameron,
you stand accused
of sorcerous
interference . . .

General Greer:
Wait. Wait.
This is . . .

General Steinem:
You shut up,
unless you want to
be tried with him.
Sorcerous
interference.
Verdict?

General Dworkin:
Guilty.

General Greer:
Innocent.

General Steinem:
Sorcerous
interference.
Verdict?

General Dworkin:
Guilty.

General Greer:
Innocent.
If you'll just let
me say one . . .

General Steinem:
We can't permit
you to interfere
and violate the
clear parameters
of rendering a
decision.
I repeat.
Sorcerous
interference.
Verdict?

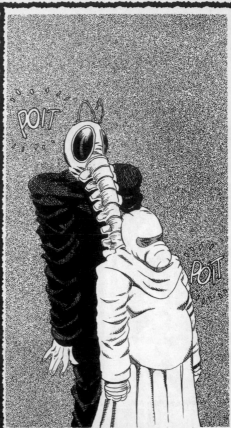
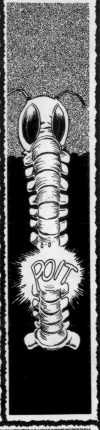

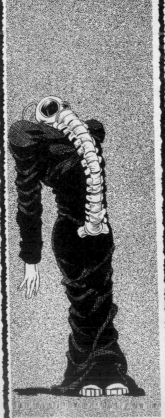

138

POIT!

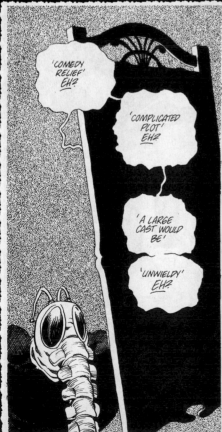

'COMEDY RELIEF' EH?

'COMPLICATED PLOT' EH?

'A LARGE CAST WOULD BE'

'UNWIELDY' EH?

I'LL SHOW YOU 'UNWIELDY'...

POKE POKE

RAK RAK

TINI

139

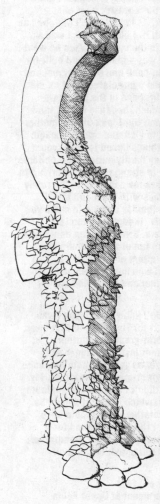

I am an old woman, of course, and so the various threats of punishment by our beloved government bother me not in the least. You are quite young however and so I suggest that you destroy this letter after you read it.

The answer to your question is that it just happened. Almost all of our men-folk were killed in the last great invasion by the Sepran Empire; either in the war itself or at the time of their withdrawal to within the borders of Lower Felda. We were raised to be ladies and with all of the natural obedience and politeness that that entails. How could we resist someone like Cirin? We had survived the Sepran occupation with our heads bowed and now that they were gone we had traded one military dictatorship for another. To be honest, I don't think any of us had considered that it would last. There was more food for the babies, fewer rapes; it was hard to see where that was so bad. But we had lost something vital. Back before the Cirinists; before the occupation by the Seprans (I'm so old, you know, I'm one of the few who can remember back that far) there was a balance and, truth be told, that balance favoured the women. Your great-great grandfather and I lived the same way that everyone else did. The men-folk had their work and they worked hard. Life wasn't easy, but we always had food on the table and not one of our five children ever went hungry. The women worked hard, too, make no mistake. But the men worked in competition with each other; some getting richer and some getting poorer and it would take its toll. I watched your great-great grandfather get old almost overnight when the trade routes started to change and they started the whole idea of tariffs in Iest and Palnu. He couldn't do a thing about it and it hurt his pride and he had to work even harder to bring in the same money he had before. My life, a woman's life, was a regular thing; like a monk or a priest, you see. The work occupied my time and my attention, but it gave me an inner peace that you don't see now. I watched my children grow up and I knew all the secrets of life first-hand. It was power, but it was a quiet kind of power, the thing that keeps it all going. We weren't trying to change anything, we were just keeping it going, we were part of it. I tried to make your great-great grandfather happy, because I knew him being out all day earning our daily bread that there wasn't a lot of happiness for him. We never talked about his work. As I used to tell him, he can leave his work outside or he can sleep outside with it. I like to think I was a comfort to him. He always looked a little younger in the morning when he went to work and I felt I owed him that much. Our home was a place he had built for us and I was there to help him lay aside his burden, cook him a warm meal and let him know there was someone who cared and who appreciated what he did for me and for his children. You know, you're the first one in the family who ever asked me about the olden times? I don't say much, because I don't think it's a woman's place; that's not the way I was raised. But I look at your mother and your aunts and their children when they come to visit and that . . . magic I guess you'd call it is gone. They fight about the things I used to make your great-great grandfather leave outside at night. They hardly notice their children which is to be expected when they give them over to strangers every morning to feed and to raise. The children are cold and it makes me sad to see. The really young ones, I'll tell them stories and play silly games with them and they'll light right up and the magic getting released from them is enough to make you cry til you never stop. By the time they're five or six, though, it's too late. They're hard and they're cold, just like their mothers. Strangers can only teach them how to be good strangers, I guess. They make fun of their fathers and they run wild or they accuse each other of being traitors and threaten to turn each other in to the Cirinist soldiers outside. A girl who hasn't even had her time yet owns more than your great-great grandfather and I ever had and all they want is more.

I just sound like a cranky old woman, don't I? I didn't know how happy I was way back when because I had nothing to compare it to. They tell me that I was oppressed. When I hear the word I think of your great-great grandfather because when I hear the word, I picture a burden that just gets bigger and bigger as you go along, a big weight that gets bigger as your strength begins to fail and finally it just crushes you. That was your great-great grandfather. My burden got lighter. The children grew up and they didn't need me every minute of every day like they did when they were younger, which is how it should be. With what they tell me now, your great-great grandfather and I should have both been carrying these enormous burdens and let the children fend for themselves. Your aunts and your mother are like your great-great grandfather; old before their time with these great weights on their shoulders as their strength begins to

Trial evidence   1411
Cirinist Government of Upper Felda
verdict: guilty
sentence: execution

Lord Julius:
How about this; "Ladies and gentlemen of the jury . . ."

Basking:
Er. It's "The Joint Upper Felda and Iest Commission on Interest Rate Policy", Lord Julius. It's not a jury.

Lord Julius:
A lot *you* know about it.

Baskin:
There won't be any 'gentlemen' is what I mean.

Lord Julius:
All right. How about; "Esteemed ladies of the Joint Upper Felda . . ."

Baskin:
They don't like to be called "ladies", Lord Julius. They consider it patronizing.

Lord Julius:
Patronizing! Don't they know an ingratiating distortion when they hear it? All right. What about; "My worthy opponents of the Joint Upper Felda . . ."

Baskin:
No no no. We want to persuade them that we're on their side; that we want to find a workable compromise.

Lord Julius:
Oh, is *that* what we want?

Baskin:
Yes. We want to show them that we're meeting with them in a spirit of cooperation and that we share their concerns.

Lord Julius:
All right. What about "Esteemed representatives of the Joint Upper Felda and Iest Commission on Interest Rate Policy."

Baskin:
Good. Very good.

Lord Julius:
"I welcome you today in a spirit of cooperation and shared concerns."

Baskin:
Very good. Go on.

Lord Julius:
I can't. I'm stuck.

Baskin:
Stuck?

Lord Julius:
Yeah. I don't know what their concerns are.

Baskin:
Their concern is that they think your interest rates are too high and they want to know the reason.

Lord Julius:
They want to know the reason? All right. "The reason that you think my interest rates are too high is that you aren't taxing your citizens enough. If you double your tax rates, my interest rates will fade to insignificance."

Baskin:
No no. They want to know the reason the interest rates are high; not the reason they *think* they're too high.

Lord Julius:
Well, tell them to make up their minds. How about this; "I share your concerns about high interest rates. For the life of me, I can't figure it out either."

Baskin:
I think they'll want more information. More specifics.

143

Lord Julius:
"Specifically, I can't figure out why they're at eighteen and a quarter per cent."

Baskin:
Perhaps. Perhaps if you could explain how you arrived at that figure.

Lord Julius:
That's just it; the number I pulled out of the hat was seventeen and a half. Listen, I can't get up any momentum with you interrupting all the time. You there. With the cereal bowl on your head. What do we have so far?

Me:
"Esteemed representatives of the Joint Upper Felda and lest Commission on Interest Rate Policy. I welcome you today in a spirit of cooperation and shared concerns. I share your concerns about high interest rates. For the life of me, I can't figure it out either. Specifically, I can't figure out why they're at eighteen and a quarter per cent . . ."

Lord Julius:
". . . when the number I pulled out of the hat was seventeen and a half. As I think about it, here before you, my suspicions are aroused. And believe me, as I look at all of you, that's the only thing that's aroused."

Baskin:
Lord Julius.

Lord Julius:
All right. Strike that last sentence. "My suspicions are aroused. Could it be that the number was actually the little ticket indicating the size of hat? For I recall, quite clearly, that the hat was unusually large . . ."

Baskin:
Lord Julius. Please. They're looking for specifics.

Lord Julius:
". . . was unusually large and of a soft gray material seldom found in sub-temperate climates. As I consider this now, a great deal seems to hinge on the size of head of the hat's owner. Further, since at no time did I see the figures marked on any of the other slips of paper, it is impossible for me to say with any degree of certainty whether the number in question was high relative to the other numbers or low. Moreover, there is still the question of how seventeen and a half per cent became eighteen and a quarter per cent; a question which concerns all of us here today."

Baskin:
Good. Good. Keep going.

Lord Julius:
"Thank you for your time and attention and I hope you enjoy the petit fours and watery lemonade on sale in the foyer."

Baskin:
Lord Julius.

Lord Julius:
"A question which concerns all of us here today. In the interests of cooperation and shared concern I propose therefore that you join me in merging the "Palnan Executive Commission on Floating Interest Rate Policy" and your own "Joint Upper Felda and lest Commission on Interest Rate Policy" into a new and more effective "Double-Jointed Upper Felda/lest and Palnu Commission on Interest Rate Reduction and Fiscal Responsibility". As a concrete demonstration of my solemn commitment to this vital issue, I will authorize an immediate doubling of each commission member's salary, tripling of the commission's operating budget, the quadrupling of the commission's research and support staff and . . ." What's 'times five' again?

Baskin:
Quintupling.

Lord Julius:
". . . and quintupling of the current allocation of office space and office decoration budget. Furthermore, I will sign into law tomorrow a proclamation giving the new Double-Jointed Commission a free hand, an open door and a clean slate for a period of not less than two years, ensuring that its examination of the issue will be as thorough and as all-encompassing as possible; at the conclusion of which, the commission's report will be submitted to the three governments participating for swift and decisive examination and discussion with an eye toward full implementation within an appropriate time-frame."

Baskin:
Perfect.

Lord Julius:
Have the boys at State throw in a few warm reminiscences at the end there about Palnu's long and happy association with those meddlesome vultures.

Baskin:
Yes, Lord Julius.

Lord Julius:
Hang that big ugly picture of Cirin behind the podium; make sure it's high enough so you can't see the holes the darts made.

Baskin:
Yes, Lord Julius.

Y'U LUK TARRABOOL MEESTER CEREBOOS THE PUP

AYE... THAT SMALL BUCKET OF SCOTCH WENT DOWN THE WRONG WAY LAST NIGHT ...

SO!

WHAD WU'D Y'U LIKE FOOR BRAGEFOOST? ...

ANOTHER BUCKET OF SCOTCH...

MAKE IT A LARGE ONE THIS TIME

RRIGHT AHWHAY...

WHY-- MISS JAKA!

YOU'VE HARDLY TOUCHED YOUR BREAKFAST ...

MISS JAKA?

General
Steinem:
Great Cirin!

Cirin:
Dreams.
Dreams and
reality.

General
Greer:
You're awake.

Cirin:
Yes. No.
Wakefulness
is the issue.
The dreams
and reality
are merging.
The first act
of violence.
The first and
the last.
It must be.

General
Greer:
We thought
that you . . .

Cirin:
Quiet. I must
say these
things. They
must be writ-
ten down.
Wakefulness.
Focus.
Division must
be resisted.
There's a
contradiction.
Extreme
focus means
that much is
lost in the
periphery.
In seeing
the overall
picture, detail
is lost. It is
summed up
in those two
things. The
dismissal of
contrary view-
points brings
division.
Is that
inevitable?
Accommo-
dation without
corruption.
The two
queens
crush the
manifestation
of the dream.
They grow
larger and
if that contin-
ues unabated,
the bishops
will prevail.
Inactivity
is their
strength.
Stasis serves
their purpose.
Awareness.
Unawareness.
Dream.
Reality.
Presented as
a problem.
Whom shall
stasis serve
when . . .?

Cirin:
My arm. What is this? What has happened?

General Steinem:
Great Cirin . . .

Cirin:
Quiet. Quiet. The chariot. The chariot a carriage. The Tower falls. Motion and discord. All must be calm. Stasis can serve us as well. Calm and understanding; an accommodation. Yes it is time. It must be time. The Goddess pulls aside her mask and has two faces. Heresy. Heresy to one or both. The impurities can only be that which divides us. What is left to us when the disagreements are set aside? The Goddess speaks of accommodation to us both. All else must fall away like a snake shedding its skin. Calm. Stasis. Our momentum can carry us, but we must let the divisiveness fall away. And what aids our cause? What brings about this accommodation?

148

General Greer: Everything is being written down.

Cirin: Yes. Yes. You are here as well, aren't you. You are my dream and my reality. I could hear you. You have a single voice. The others who are here. No one must speak. No questions. A delicate balance in the border between wakefulness and dream, as fine as the web of a spider. The one who just spoke. Who said that everything is being written down. Stay. Stay by me. The others must leave. Now. Quietly. I will discuss all of this with you later. For now the connection must be maintained and it is fragile. Leave me. Leave me now.

Cirin:
The stenographer stayed as well. That is indeed our strength. Everything is being written down. And you are calm. I can feel it. The transcriptions and how we have used them. You know, don't you? They are a strength and yet so much has been lost. I began to rely on summaries. I was eaves-dropping on my own sycophants. Allowing them ...no, honesty now ... encouraging them to flatter me. How long since I have reviewed a conversation that troubled me; that raised doubt? What is between the lines; what is the subtext? What was actually being said? How tempting to request only summaries; a few para-graphs of empty flattery, idle gossip. All that would cause offense to me was excluded, stripped away and hidden from me. Like a man. Very like a man.

General Greer:
I've ... thought that.

Cirin:
Yes, and then censored yourself out of loyalty; the implied requirement of my retreat into dreams; into reality manu-factured and ... foolish. So very foolish.

It *is* calm, now. Can we sus-tain this? Our voices are like two parts of the same melody. How wonderful. Do you hear her? Do you hear her voice?

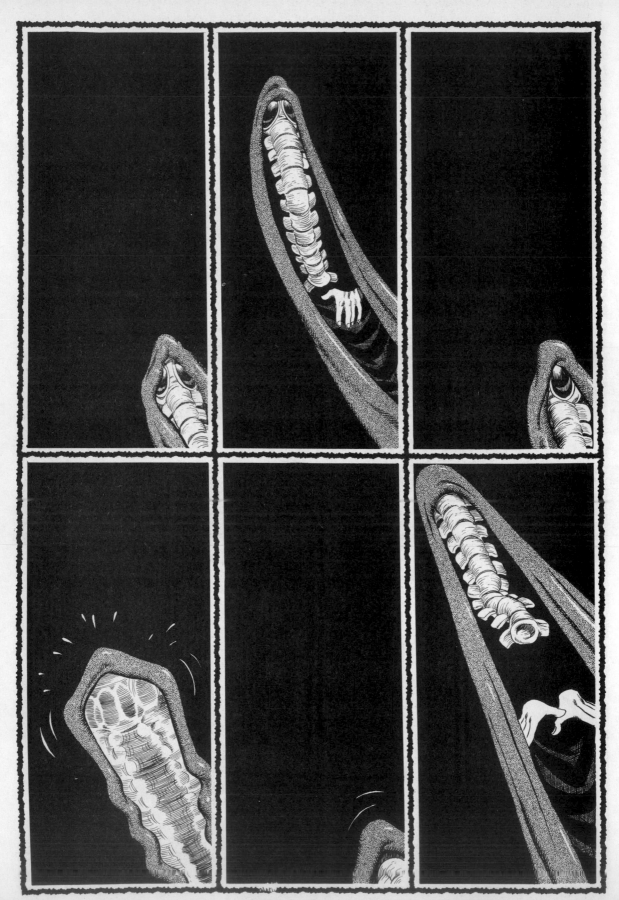

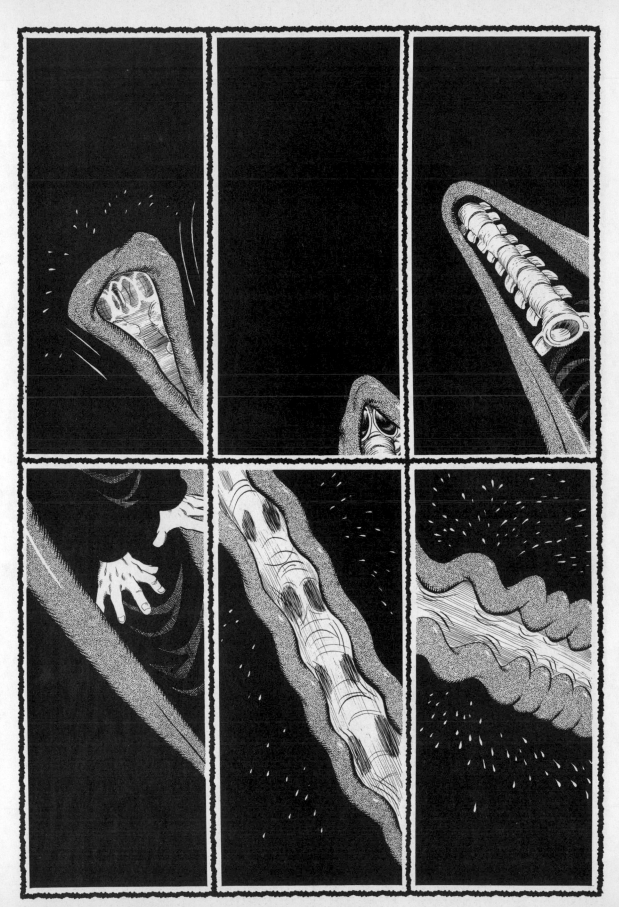

156

158

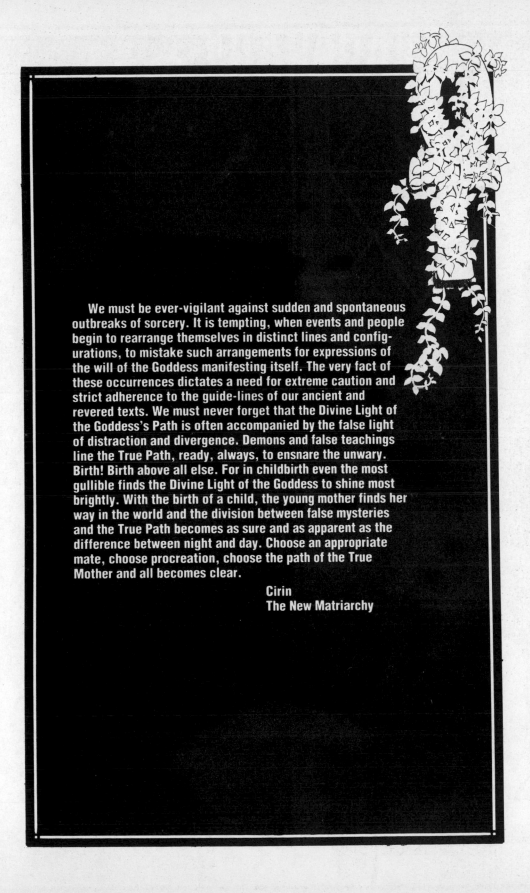

We must be ever-vigilant against sudden and spontaneous outbreaks of sorcery. It is tempting, when events and people begin to rearrange themselves in distinct lines and configurations, to mistake such arrangements for expressions of the will of the Goddess manifesting itself. The very fact of these occurrences dictates a need for extreme caution and strict adherence to the guide-lines of our ancient and revered texts. We must never forget that the Divine Light of the Goddess's Path is often accompanied by the false light of distraction and divergence. Demons and false teachings line the True Path, ready, always, to ensnare the unwary. Birth! Birth above all else. For in childbirth even the most gullible finds the Divine Light of the Goddess to shine most brightly. With the birth of a child, the young mother finds her way in the world and the division between false mysteries and the True Path becomes as sure and as apparent as the difference between night and day. Choose an appropriate mate, choose procreation, choose the path of the True Mother and all becomes clear.

Cirin
The New Matriarchy

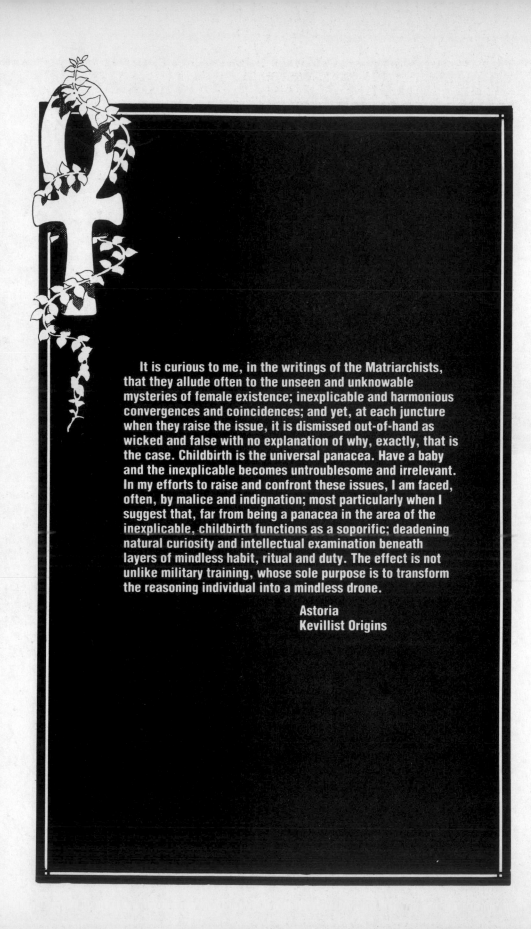

It is curious to me, in the writings of the Matriarchists, that they allude often to the unseen and unknowable mysteries of female existence; inexplicable and harmonious convergences and coincidences; and yet, at each juncture when they raise the issue, it is dismissed out-of-hand as wicked and false with no explanation of why, exactly, that is the case. Childbirth is the universal panacea. Have a baby and the inexplicable becomes untroublesome and irrelevant. In my efforts to raise and confront these issues, I am faced, often, by malice and indignation; most particularly when I suggest that, far from being a panacea in the area of the inexplicable, childbirth functions as a soporific; deadening natural curiosity and intellectual examination beneath layers of mindless habit, ritual and duty. The effect is not unlike military training, whose sole purpose is to transform the reasoning individual into a mindless drone.

Astoria
Kevillist Origins

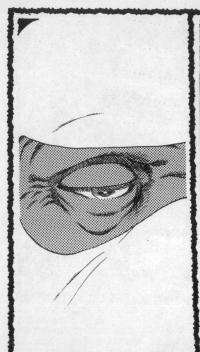

GREER.

Cirin:
I will make this short and to the point, since many events are beginning to converge and time is of the essence. I have just read the transcript of our conversation earlier; just after I awoke from my coma. I was obviously feverish and I babbled some nonsense about information being kept from me; which, of course, we both know is not true. It is the very essence of our movement that all information is exchanged freely, that it is assessed carefully and its application is measured and just. And yet, I see here that you seem to feel that I have the traits of a man.

General Greer:
I . . .

Cirin:
In my fever, I said 'Like a man. Very like a man.' To which you reply, 'I've thought of that.' Do you deny it?

General Greer:
No, Great Cirin. In the context of . . . what I thought you were . . .

Cirin:
And do you realize that the expression of such a view represents an extremely serious form of treason against the Goddess herself?

General Greer:
Great Cirin, in the context of the conversation . . .

Cirin:
Just answer the question.

General Greer:
I . . . yes, Great Cirin.

165

Cirin: General Greer, you are hereby found guilty of high treason against the Goddess and against the occupational government of Iest. You are to be taken from this place and executed within the hour. May the Goddess have mercy upon your soul.

166

 VEN BEFORE HIS HEAD hit the tavern floor, Cerebus was asleep and dreaming. It was odd, though, because he was aware of lying on the tavern floor and aware that he was dreaming at the same time. His hands were gripping a railing of some kind and he was staring out across cloud formations unlike any he had ever seen. They had equal characteristics of clouds and of ocean waves; rising and rolling too slowly to be composed of water, but too quickly and in patterns too regular to be cloud-like. Plying its way through the cloud-waves was an ornate sofa and endtable, beneath a crescent moon ringed by three stars in a cloudless sky. There was a small figure bobbing up and down in the cloud-waves who resembled an insect, shouting for help.

'Help! I'm being held captive in my sister's...'

The rest of his words were lost in a thunderous rush of cloud-wave and he vanished from view.

At that moment, a figure appeared, perched on the arm of the sofa, drink in hand, clad only in under-garments. Astoria. Cerebus recognized her instantly; and as he gazed at her profile, it was as if he could read her thoughts as she gazed straight ahead at...

HE CHURCH. SHE'S UP there right now. She severed the link; willfully, without a moment's hesitation or regret. What possibility is there now? All we can do is to act out the same events in the same sequence. What made her this way? How could she see something so clearly; speak the words in rhythm with me; and then turn her back and resume her old ways? Compromise was possible. With both of our minds we could have made it happen. There's every reason to think that we wouldn't even have had to take any action. If we could just let things take their course and resist the urge to destroy each other. But she's the destroyer. Isn't she? I'm the one who's going to be on trial. There's something there, Astoria, old girl. Don't lose it now. She's the destroyer. That's wrong. Even when I thought that, it was as if something was squeezing my heart. We're both destroyers. We both seek destruction.

I seek destruction.

Is that it? No. But it's part of it. And that's the part I can change. If I don't try to bring about her destruction. If I can see where she's right and where I'm wrong. Even without a link between us, I can still change myself and attempt to influence events. My followers. I can feel them peering at me through the latice-work doors. Their minds filled with questions. Of course, I *am* sitting on the arm of a sofa in my underwear sipping scotch.

Time to get dressed.

After fuming about his know-it-all wise-guy evil twin for some time and puzzling over the inexplicable transformation of his appearance, George (I am not the Judge) at last began to feel a strange and unprecedented calm descend upon him. His gaze rose above the Moon's horizon just as the Sun slipped from view and the stars began to shine in the night sky. For the first time in the uncounted centuries of his observation, he could see, and what was more, understand. His lips parted slightly and he stood there through the long night witnessing and understanding. 'I was wrong,' he thought, more than once. 'I was wrong.' The colour drained gradually from his face and as the sun rose once more, behind him, he felt a single tear form in his right eye. 'I'm sorry', he said then. 'I'm so sorry.'

Cirin:
I have reviewed the transcripts from our people keeping Cerebus under observation in the Lower City; most particularly the time immediately prior to and immediately subsequent to the collapsing of the mountain on the Regency Hotel.

General Steinem:
Yes, Great Cirin?

Cirin:
I want them all recalled to duty here in the Upper City and replaced. Immediately. They've either lost their minds or, more likely, they are Illusionist infiltrators. Have you read the transcripts?

General Steinem:
No, Great Cirin. So much has been going on, I . . .

Cirin:
I'll have a set sent to your quarters. They observed him going onto the roof and raising his sword; that's all. And yet, to a one, they attributed that simple act to the completely unrelated geological shifting and collapse of the mountain.

General Steinem:
Mm. I see what you mean. Is it possible that the Illusionists themselves, by some means of mesmerization or . . .

Cirin:
I thought of that. It seems more likely that someone with a vested interest in Cerebus being something more than a mishappen little drunkard infiltrated. That's why I want all of them recalled. And make sure they're all replaced by second and third generation Upper Feldans; no Iestans.

General Steinem:
Yes, Great Cirin.

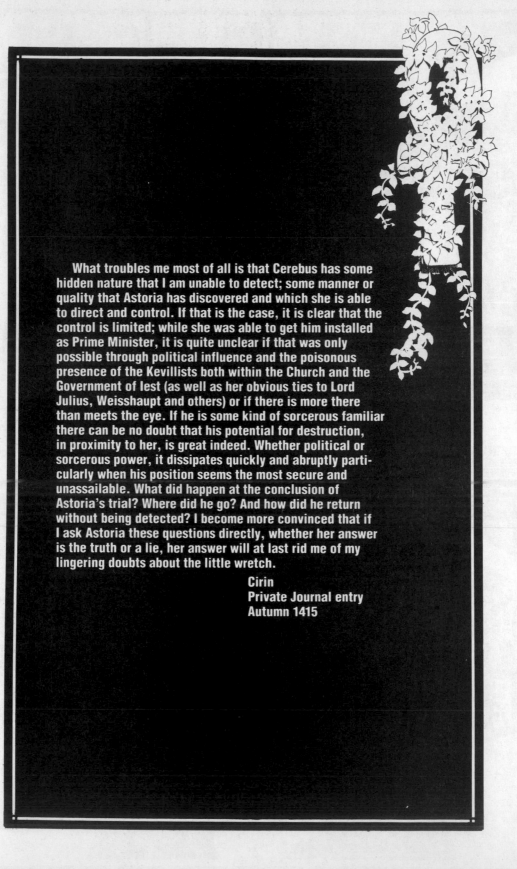

What troubles me most of all is that Cerebus has some hidden nature that I am unable to detect; some manner or quality that Astoria has discovered and which she is able to direct and control. If that is the case, it is clear that the control is limited; while she was able to get him installed as Prime Minister, it is quite unclear if that was only possible through political influence and the poisonous presence of the Kevillists both within the Church and the Government of Iest (as well as her obvious ties to Lord Julius, Weisshaupt and others) or if there is more there than meets the eye. If he is some kind of sorcerous familiar there can be no doubt that his potential for destruction, in proximity to her, is great indeed. Whether political or sorcerous power, it dissipates quickly and abruptly particularly when his position seems the most secure and unassailable. What did happen at the conclusion of Astoria's trial? Where did he go? And how did he return without being detected? I become more convinced that if I ask Astoria these questions directly, whether her answer is the truth or a lie, her answer will at last rid me of my lingering doubts about the little wretch.

Cirin
Private Journal entry
Autumn 1415

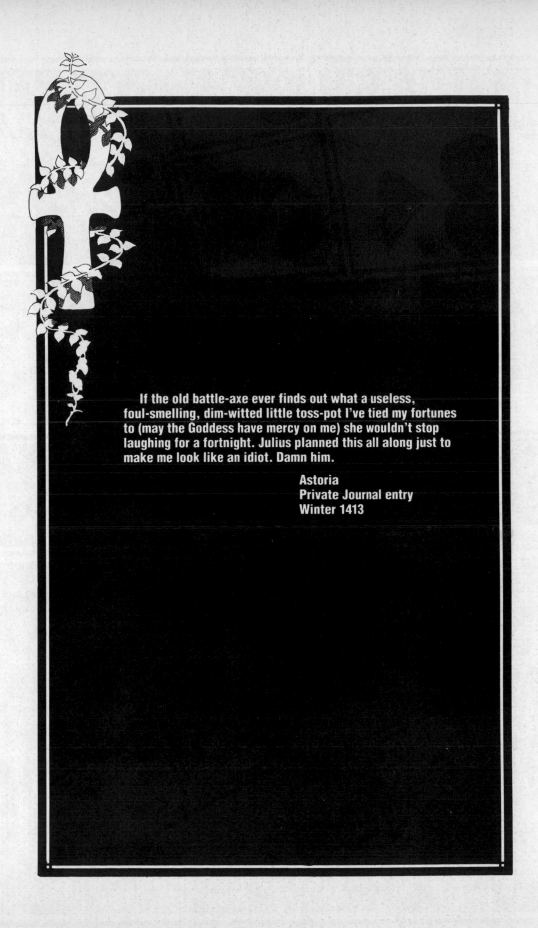

If the old battle-axe ever finds out what a useless, foul-smelling, dim-witted little toss-pot I've tied my fortunes to (may the Goddess have mercy on me) she wouldn't stop laughing for a fortnight. Julius planned this all along just to make me look like an idiot. Damn him.

Astoria
Private Journal entry
Winter 1413

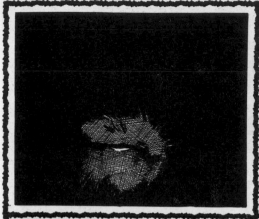

181

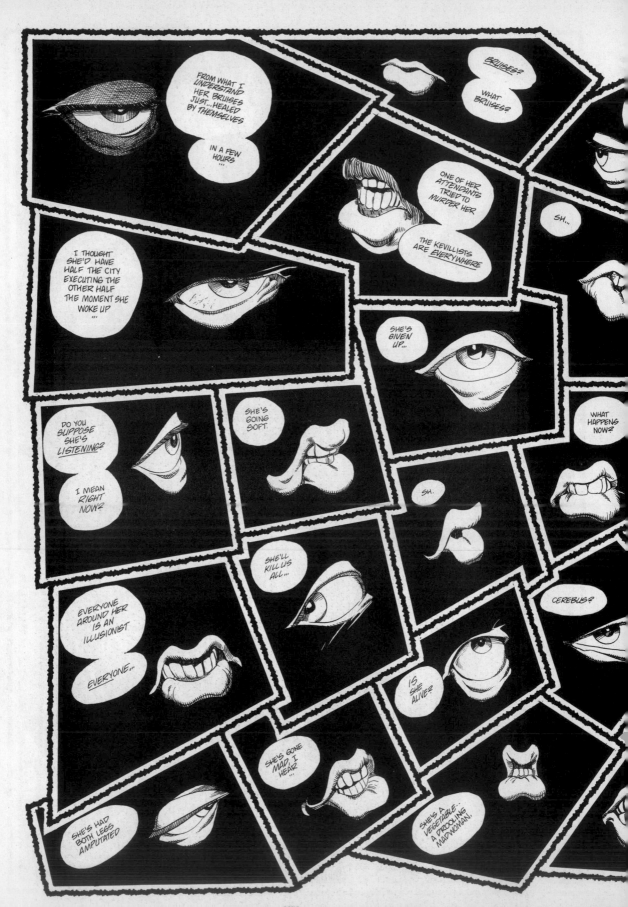

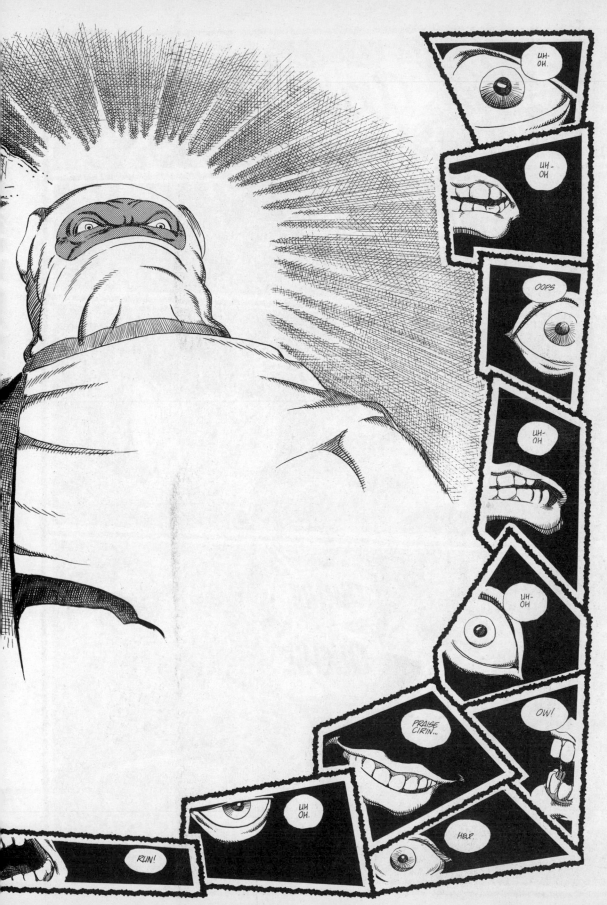

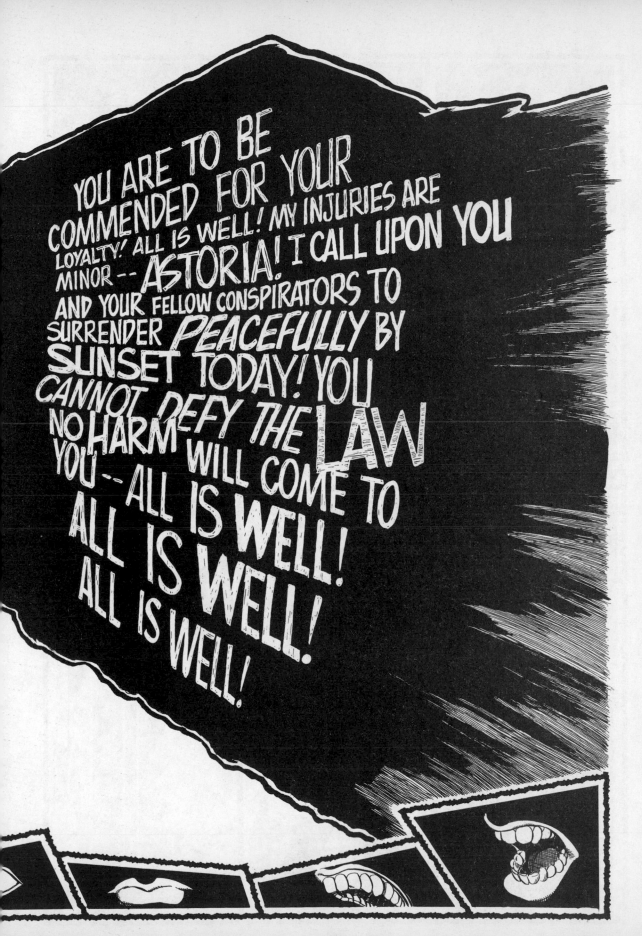

GREAT
ASTORIA?

MM.

THEY'RE
...

THEY'RE
GOING TO
KILL US

AREN'T
THEY.

YES,
THEY
ARE.

DOES
THAT
BOTHER
YOU?

WELL
YES!

I
MEAN.

NO
ONE WANTS
TO *DIE.*

ON THE CONTRARY

I'VE BEEN LOOKING FORWARD TO *MY* DEATH SINCE I WAS *EIGHT* YEARS OLD...

BUT -- YOUR *WORK*...

YOUR *MOVEMENT*.

MOVEMENT?

THIS ISN'T A *MOVEMENT* ANYMORE...

IT'S A *CHARADE*

A *FARCE*...

I SPENT *YEARS* CONSTRUCTING A CELL SYSTEM IN THIS CITY

PENETRATING ALL OF THE CRUCIAL DEPARTMENTS OF THE CHURCH *AND* THE GOVERNMENT...

I'M BROUGHT, *UNCONSCIOUS*, TO THIS HOTEL...

AND WHAT DO *YOU* DO?

YOU ALL *CONVERGE* HERE-- A FLOCK OF SITTING DUCKS...

SITTING AND WRINGING YOUR HANDS...

FRETTING.

WORRYING.

WAITING FOR *ME* TO COME UP WITH SOME MIRACULOUS MILITARY PLAN THAT WILL ALLOW A BUNCH OF *SECRETARIES* AND *STENOGRAPHERS* TO DEFEAT SEVERAL *LEGIONS* OF TRAINED *MERCENARIES*...

WELL, IT ISN'T GOING TO HAPPEN.

WE'RE GOING TO DIE.

GET USED TO IT...

B-BUT GREAT ASTORIA...

WHEN HAVE I EVER ASKED YOU TO CALL ME THAT?

YOU JUST DON'T GET IT...

ANY OF YOU

I'M NOT A DAMN QUEEN

I'M NOT A DAMN GODDESS

I AM

ASTORIA

PERIOD!

I TRIED TO TEACH YOU HOW TO LIVE LIKE HUMAN BEINGS ...STRONG... INDEPENDENT

AND OBVIOUSLY I FAILED...

GO OUT AND JOIN THE OTHERS...I'LL BE OUT AS SOON AS I'M DRESSED.

IF I CAN'T TEACH ALL OF YOU HOW TO LIVE, MAYBE I CAN TEACH YOU HOW TO DIE...

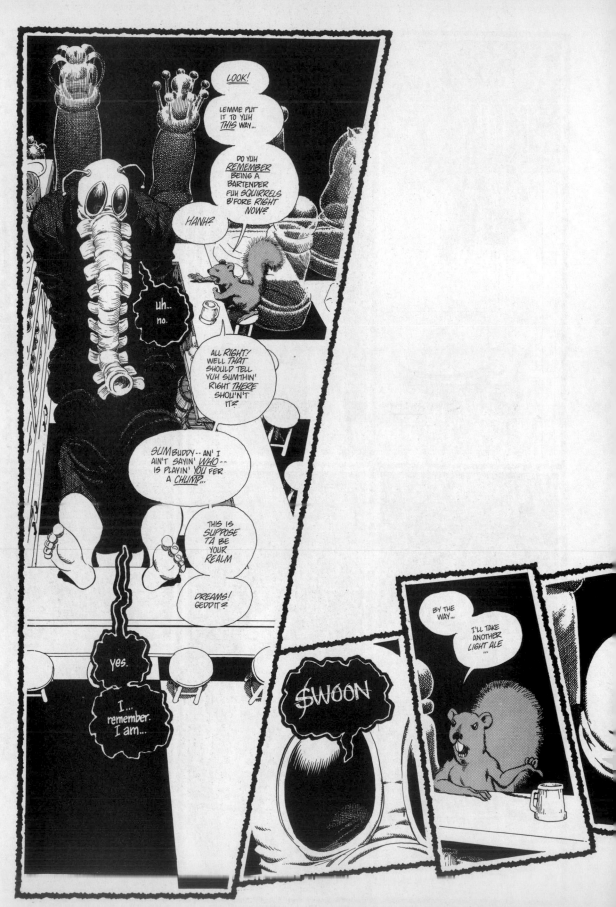

Cirin:
No no. You're flipping the pages too fast.

Dorana:
I'm sorry. Perhaps if . . .

Cirin:
No. It just isn't going to work. Let me think.

Cirin:
We'll just have to move the books themselves. All of the shelves which have been purified; move all of those books to the end of the library which faces the Ascension site. All of the shelves which haven't been purified; move all of those books to the opposite end of the library.

Dorana:
Yes, Great Cirin.

Cirin:
You'll have to work quickly. We're running out of time as it is.

Dorana:
Yes, Great Cirin.

If there was ever a more concrete example of the sheer willful and contrary nature of daughters when they are allowed to roam the corridors of power, unchecked and unfettered, it is the Eye in the Pyramid. Ostensibly based on an ancient and marginal philosophy, it amounts to little more than disobedience and rebelliousness as political theory. Fortunately the adherents of this cult are easily discovered and rooted out; a wise and organized leader has only to seek out those areas of government where information and decision-making are regularly impeded or neutralized and remove the person responsible. It is less a political movement than it is a haven for misguided pranksters.

Cirin
The New Matriarchy

The Eye in the Pyramid (unlike the ancient symbol of wisdom) is located in the middle of the pyramid, not at its apex. It applies to all hierarchical systems. As applied to Kevillism, it is an illustration of the power which resides at the so-called lower echelons of hierarchical systems. Anyone with any experience in government or business knows that those supposedly in power have only a cursory awareness of how the system operates, and a nearly complete ignorance of the day-in day-out exchange of information, book-keeping and paper-work which is its life's blood. Through my writings on the Eye in the Pyramid, I endeavour only to make secretaries, book-keepers, executive assistants and others aware that they, and not their superiors, control the levers of power. That awareness is my sole motivation and the goal I wish to achieve. What they choose to do with that awareness, once they have achieved it, is entirely up to them and of no interest to me whatsoever.

Astoria
Kevillist Origins

ALL RIGHT...

WHO KNOWS HOW MUCH LAMP OIL THERE IS IN THE HOTEL?

THE - THE HOTEL HAS GASLIGHTS...

I'M AWARE OF THAT -- THERE STILL HAS TO BE A SUPPLY

GASLIGHTS ARE FAIRLY NEW

EVERYWHERE BUT THE REGENCY.

BRING THE OIL HERE

WE'RE ALSO GOING TO NEED LARGE GLASS CONTAINERS FROM THE KITCHEN

LAMPS AS WELL

THERE ARE THREE IN MY SUITE ALONE... SO THERE SHOULD BE QUITE A FEW...

WE'RE GOING TO NEED THEM ALL -- EVERY LAST ONE

I KNOW I DON'T HAVE TO TELL YOU HOW...

ASTORIA.

WHAT?

SORRY TO INTERRUPT.

BUT I THOUGHT THE WHOLE IDEA OF THIS...

'MOVEMENT'...

...WAS TO SHARE THE DECISION-MAKING...

NO LEADERS.

NO FOLLOWERS.

NOW, IF YOU HAVE A PLAN-- I'M SURE WE'D ALL LOVE TO HEAR IT

ON THE OTHER HAND, IF YOU JUST WANT TO SNAP YOUR FINGERS...

AND HAVE EVERYONE JUST FETCH AND CARRY FOR YOU...

MAYBE YOU SHOULD HAVE STUCK WITH YOUR MALE HOUSE-PETS.

HEN SHE HAD shared her dream that morning with Cirin, this was exactly what Astoria had been able to see for the first time. The complaint was valid. Had she not just reduced a young woman to tears by insisting that she was not a queen, not a goddess? and yet here she was, striding about the room, barking commands, using her personal magnetism, her charisma to sweep these women along a chosen path. She could feel all eyes in the room upon her, awaiting her answer. All her ideals and the newly-awakened awareness of her own folly wanted, simply, to agree. 'Yes. You're quite right,' she wanted to say, 'Let's sit down and discuss our options.' But even as the thought came, she knew that was not what she would say. Already she felt herself swept into the momentum of events; the irresistible tide of disaster which loomed before them all. She was not helpless to affect the outcome; in point of fact she was choosing helplessness. Despite her protests, she *was* a leader and even as she assessed all the inherent contradictions; the rightness of the woman who had dared to challenge her authority, the hypocrisy of her own position; her mind was weighing a variety of replies; not on the basis of what was right, but rather on the basis of what was expeditious; what would produce the proper effect. She was simultaneously amused and appalled that the proper effect she sought was blind and unquestioning obedience. A mere handful of seconds had passed, but all her experience told her that the balance of opinion in the room was very much in favour of obedience. Had she felt the momentum shifting in favour of this newcomer, she would have thrown a tantrum (as well as some heavy and fragile artifact at a key moment in her monologue as a kind of punctuation). The fear in the room, however, was her greatest asset at this point. Her reply needed to be calm, deliberate and succinct. It needed only an undertone of blame; only a suggestion that she, Astoria, could yet save the day and her followers' fear would do the rest. Her followers. If she was not a queen or a goddess, why did she always refer to them as followers? With practiced ease, she shifted her weight from her heels to the balls of her feet and began to speak.

YES. OF COURSE.

IDEALLY THAT WAS THE WAY THINGS *SHOULD* WORK

OF COURSE *IDEALLY* ALL OF YOU SHOULDN'T HAVE FLOCKED TO THIS HOTEL

IDEALLY YOU SHOULD STILL BE MANIPULATING IEST FROM *WITHIN*...

ANONYMOUSLY.

SOME OF YOU STILL *ARE*...

THOSE WHO HAVE CHOSEN TO GATHER AROUND ME...

...HOWEVER...

WILL JUST HAVE TO TRUST THAT I'M MAKING THE *RIGHT* CHOICES.

UNLESS

OF COURSE

YOU WANT TO *PERSUADE* US ALL TO FOLLOW *YOU*...

LET ME KNOW WHEN YOU HAVE EVERYTHING TOGETHER...

I'LL BE IN MY SUITE...

VINTAGE ASTORIA performance, she thought wryly to herself. Her face was a mask, composed in equal measure of concern, decisiveness and introspection. She retreated slowly but could see that she had achieved her goal. Some of her followers looked at her with awe; those were the ones who were the most afraid. Some smiled, knowingly; those were the ones who identified with her. To them, the dismissal of the newcomer was a victory which they shared with her. Some of them (very very few) could see that she had evaded, not answered the charge. They were the most intelligent. They would wrestle with the contradiction internally; their loyalty and their idealism in a perfect stasis. Loyalty would place them firmly and comfortably within the newly-reinforced consensus. Idealism would force them to side with the discredited minority viewpoint. If any discussion ensued in her absence, Astoria knew they would adopt a wait-and-see position. Carefully, deliberately, she opened the door to her suite, and then closed it behind her.

SHE LISTENED briefly as the quiet murmur of voices began outside. She thought of the faces that she had seen. The young ones trying to look old. The old ones trying to look young. Girls, Women. Ladies. There was still time to change course. She could walk back out and explain that she was tired of rhetorical sleight-of-hand; ask them what it was *they* wanted to do. Ask them what *she* should do. The newcomer and the ones who could see the verbal games-manship for what it was. What would they say? Whatever they would say, she thought to herself, I would have a pat answer. And that pat answer would point them towards blind and unquestioning obedience. The voices outside the door subsided. In her minds' eye Astoria could see flames consuming the hotel.

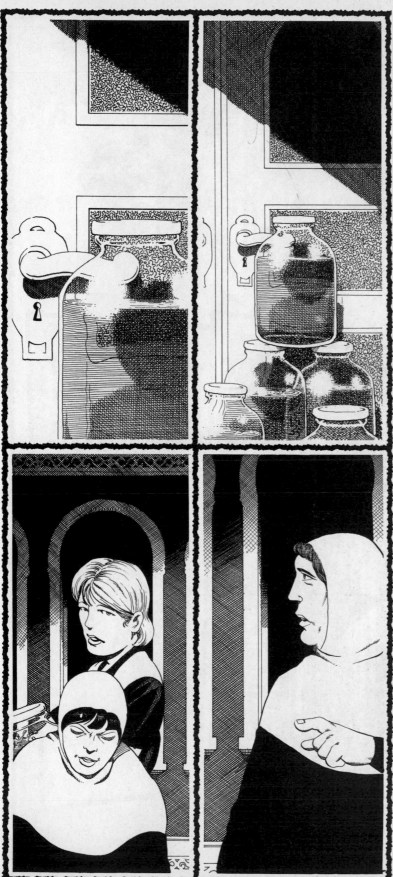

IME PASSED like wet sand through an hour-glass. She had to keep them all busy; their attentions focussed on minutiae. If they stopped working, they would start thinking and if they started thinking they would realize that she intended a mass suicide by fire. She moved swiftly from place to place; praising the mindless enterprise of the blindly obedient; discussing impossible strategies with the intelligent and the insightful. Their complete lack of military background was her greatest asset. Astoria knew that Cirin's troops surrounded them and would strike at every entrance simultaneously. It was, however, an easy matter to persuade her 'defenders' that the attack would center on a single entrance and that they had only to set a fire there and they would be able to escape under cover of flames, smoke and confusion. Whenever one of them would grow quiet and contemplative, she would hug them to her with her good arm and say firmly, 'the Goddess is with us'. As the sun began its descent toward the horizon she instructed the most obedient to begin preparing a large meal and to clean and scrub the main foyer. She raced back and forth from entrance to entrance. 'The Goddess is with us', 'the Goddess is with us'.

It wouldn't be long, now.

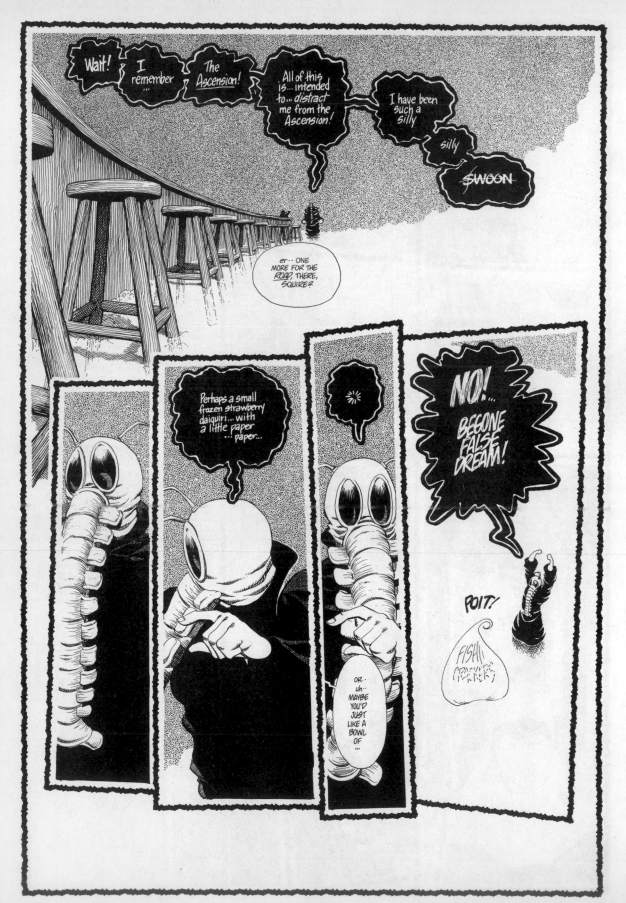

208

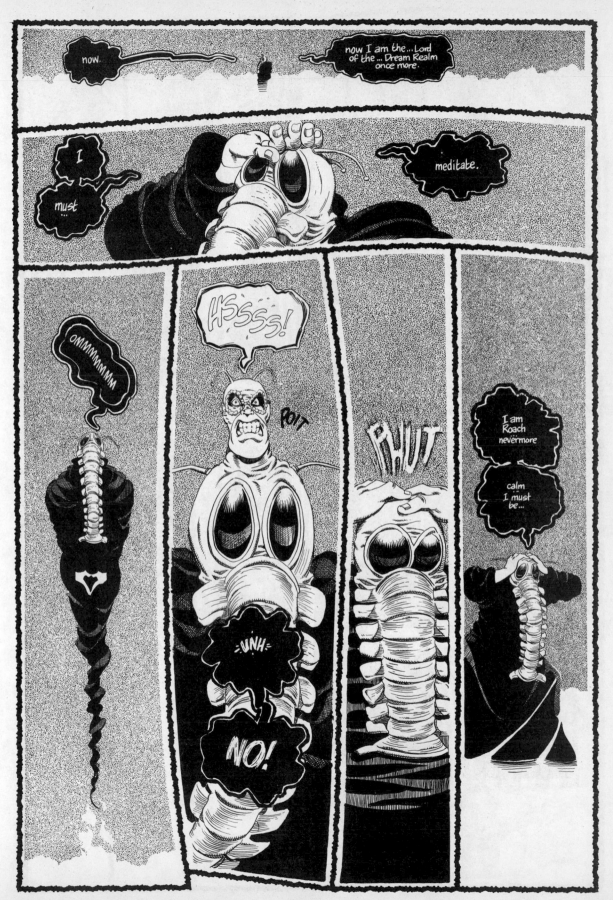

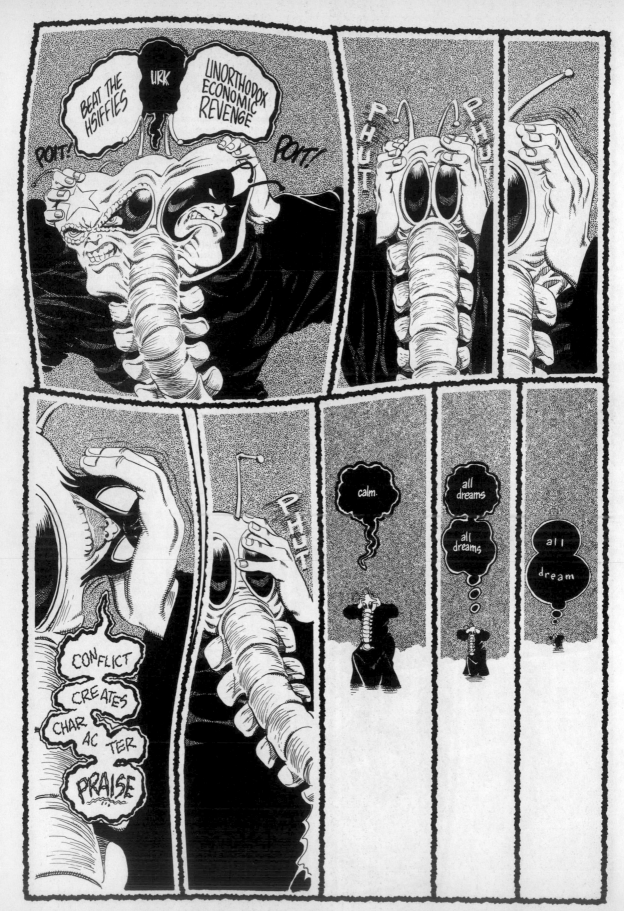

 EREBUS HAD BEEN
wide awake for some time. He felt no ill
effects from his drunken binge. He heard
the voice of Magus Doran; their final
conversation over two decades before.

'You have been my least successful pupil
and yet I am as certain today as I was the
day you came here that Tarim has chosen you as his
champion. When the time is right you will hear these words
again. The priestesses and the queens seek to steal the
magic and make it their own. Throughout history they have
controlled, manipulated, contained and infected pure male
magic. It is not theirs. It is ours! They are the soil in which
the plant grows but they are not the plant itself. Left
unchecked they will take over the churches, the armies,
businesses and government. They won't stop until their
malignancy; their poison has infected every corner of
human society. They're mad. Every one of them. Follow
insanity back to its source and you'll find a woman every
time. When you hear these words again, there will be a
throne that is rightfully yours and which you have lost
through the poisonous interference of womankind. Take it
back. You will have with you a symbol, a small token of
female poison which will represent a dead memory and
which has kept you weak. Put it aside.

You must be strong to redeem all the men who are weak.
Tarim will guide you and assist you. But it is your strength
alone which will turn the tide. You must save our magic
in the name of the Living Tarim. It can live for the first
time, free and unfettered if you are strong. Cast out the
female poisons that have kept us oppressed and bound
throughout all of human history.

> *Here's the bird that never flew.*
> *Here's the tree that never grew.*
> *Here's the bell that never rang.*
> *Here's the fish that never swam.*

It is the legend of Ketigern, the mage patron of the city of
your father's birth.

Redeem us, young Cerebus.

Redeem us.'

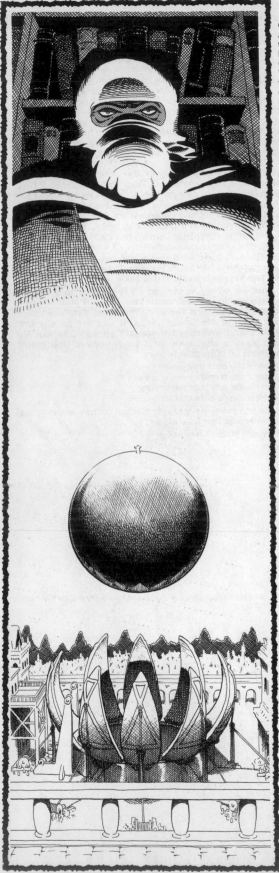

General Cho:
All of our troops in the Lower City, Great Cirin. We're . . . there are a few exceptions but we are receiving nothing but discordant imagery, fantasies. We're . . .

Cirin:
What are you saying?

General Cho:
They're all asleep, Great Cirin. They're dreaming.

Cirin:
What about Swoon Country? What about Cerebus?

General Cho:
Great Cirin, we don't know. Our people are asleep. I've just . . .

Cirin:
Why wasn't I informed of this? Damn your eyes, I said . . .

General Cho:
Great Cirin it just happened. Just this minute. I told you immediately; as soon as I was certain.

Cirin:
All right. All right. Seal the Upper City. The gold is being poured right now. Whoever is behind this they're too late. We've won. Give the order.

General Cho:
Yes, Great Cirin.

213

AND THEN ASTORIA had a vision. There she was in the park near her parents' home. She was dressed for church, but as had been her habit she had gone to the park to fantasize about her *own* church that she would build one day; a courtyard open to the skies with wild flowers growing all around. In place of an altar there would be an ornate bowl filled with exotic seeds and berries to attract beautiful and rare birds. People would talk to each other instead of listening to the droning voice of a tedious old . . .

A man had approached her. Even at that age (nine? ten?) she had had no fear of men. As he sat down beside her she had fixed him with a direct and level gaze. Without preamble he had handed her a small book with a single name; 'Kevil' engraved on its binding. 'Here' he had said. Without a word of acknowledgement she had flipped to the first page and had begun to read. An inner peace descended over her as the words appeared before her again.

> *"Wither shall we go? Shall we debate*
> *   in valley or on peak?*
> *Where shall we dwell? In what nobler*
> *   land than the isle of sunset?*
> *Where else shall we walk in peace*
> *   to and fro, on fertile ground?*
> *Who but I can take you to where*
> *   the stream runs, or falls,*
> *   clearest?"*

She had reread the passage several times; each word had seemed so sweet, so sublime, so perfect and pure.

'How much do you want for it,' she had asked, hoping the price would be less than the three copper bits tucked inside her white cotton glove; money which her mother had intended for the church collection plate. But even as she looked up, her little face solemn and determined, the man was gone. Without bothering to look around for him, she began reading. She hadn't looked up again until she had difficulty distinguishing the printed words in front of her. She realized, then, that the sun had already set and night was fast approaching.

Hiding the book in her underwear, she had hurried home.

217

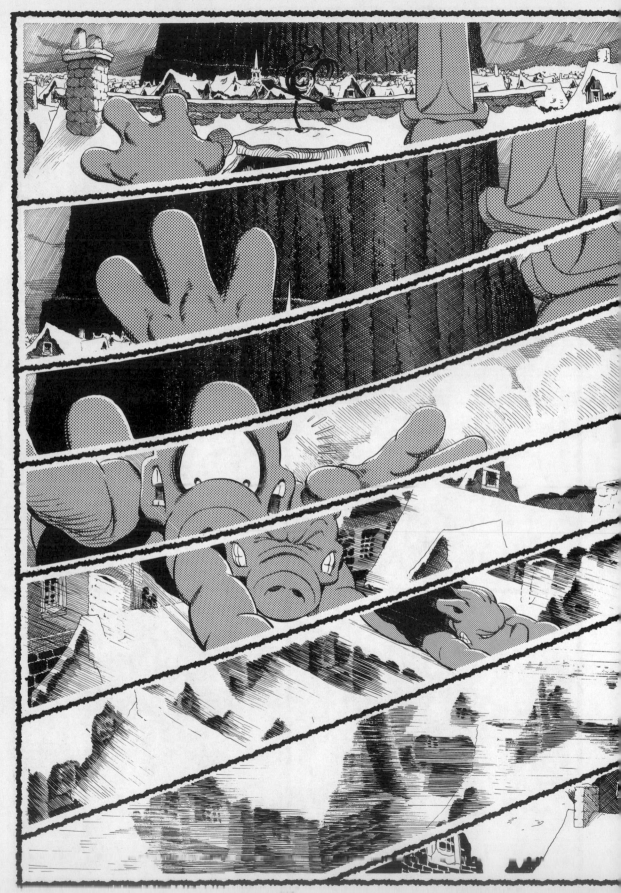

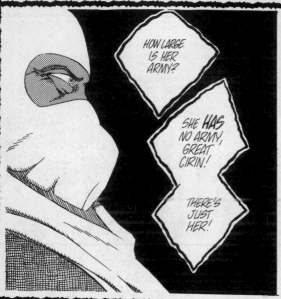

HOW LARGE IS HER ARMY?

SHE **HAS** NO ARMY, GREAT CIRIN!

THERE'S JUST HER!

GREAT CIRIN!

SHE HAS REACHED THE CENTRAL BOULEVARD!

WHAT ARE YOUR INSTRUCTIONS?

~~PLEASE!~~

calm

calm

calm

calm

223

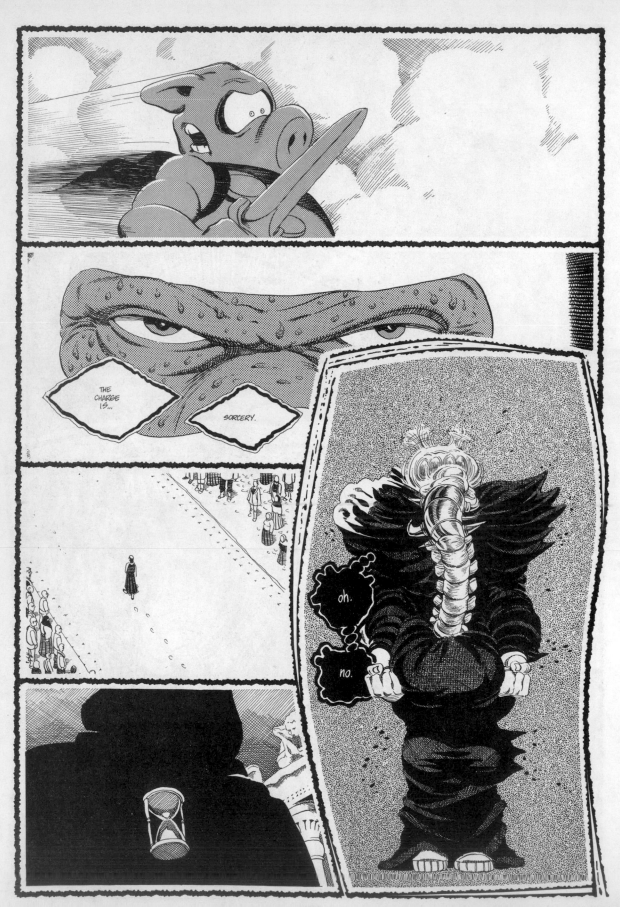

224

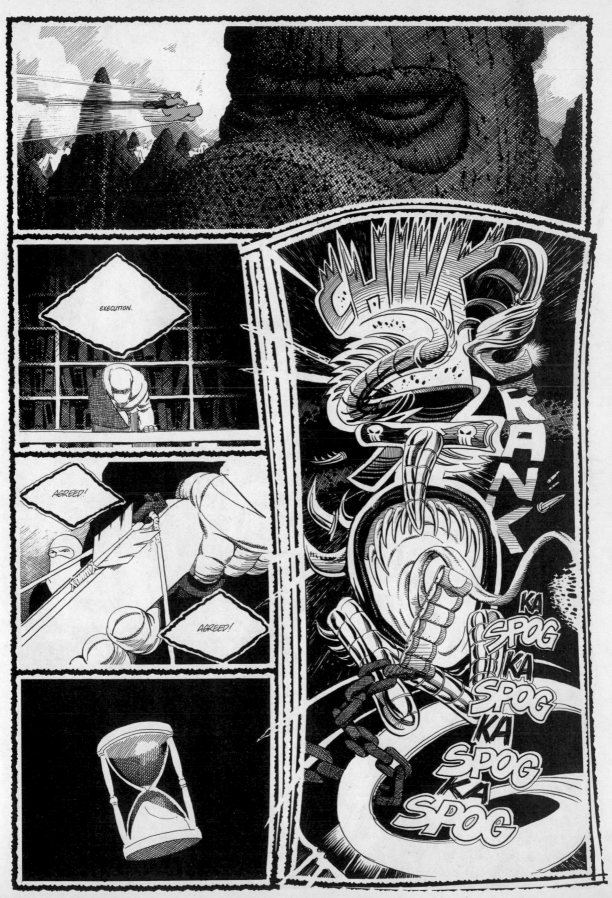

227

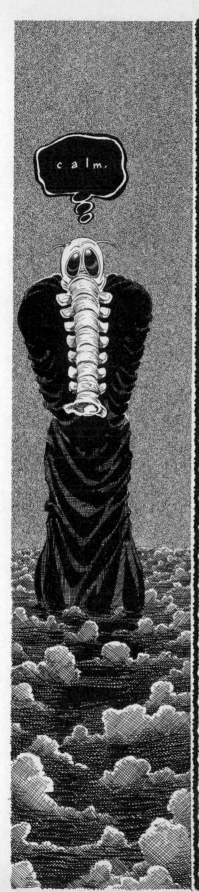

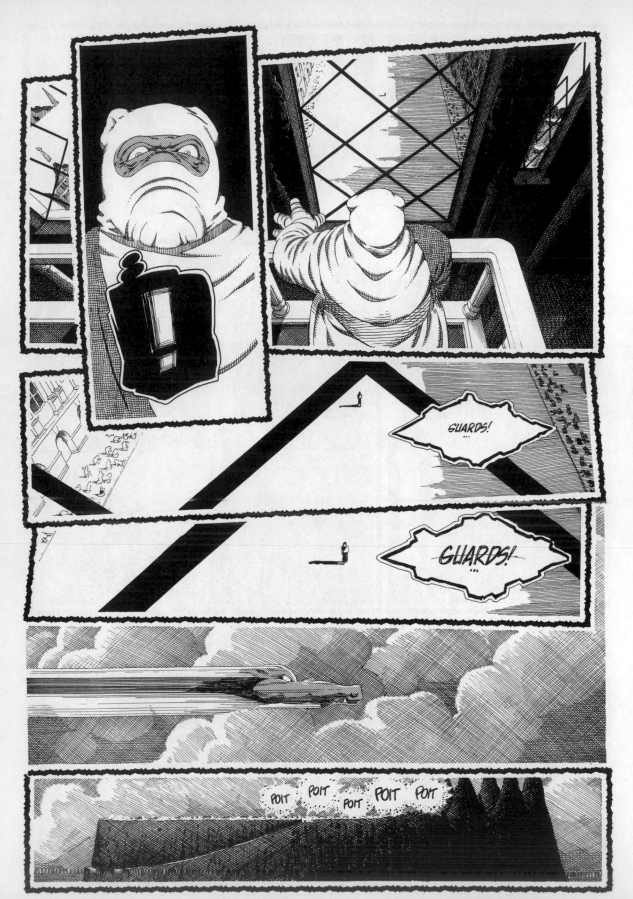

235

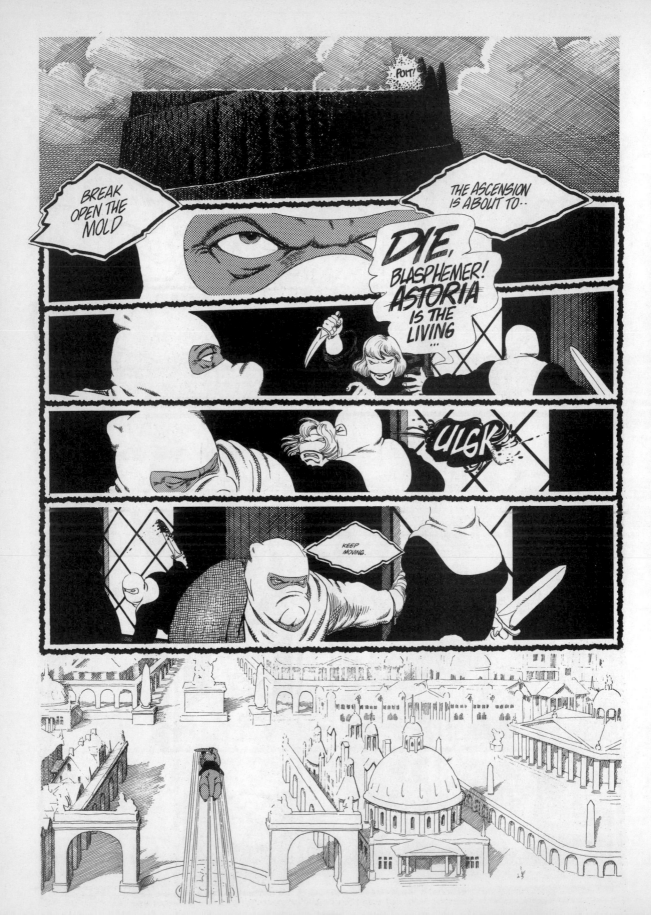

POIT!

PFUF

HAS THE MOLD BEEN OPENED?! WE'RE... ALMOST

GREAT CIRIN! ONE SIDE OF THE SPHERE... IT IT'S COLLAPSED

THE -- THE SPHERE IT'S... FLAWED.

SO.

SO THAT'S IT...

WE'RE BEATEN.

ASTORIA...

240

242

PLEASE
FORGIVE MY
MELODRAMATIC
...
DISGUISE.

I'M AFRAID
IT WAS THE
ONLY WAY
FOR ME...

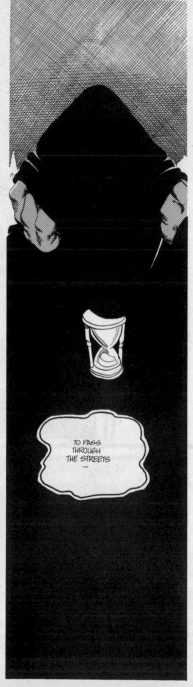

TO PASS
THROUGH
THE STREETS
...

UNMOLESTED.

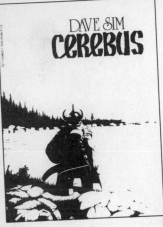
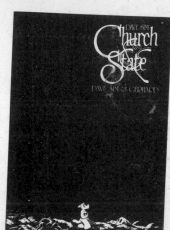

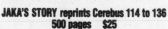